I AM THERE
Armenia

By Olivia Puccini

ISBN: 978-1469936666

Printed in the United States of America
1st Printing

Editors: Christa Banister, Leslie Linneweh and Nick Puccini
Cover Design: Casey Burres
Typesetting: Dena Swenson
Author Photo: Oliver Rõõmus

Dedication

This book is dedicated to my grandparents
Roger & Grace Crowell and Juanita Linneweh.

Thank you for being this little girl's biggest cheerleaders
and such a loving influence. Your investment in me,
as a person, will never be forgotten.

Author's Note

In the Fall of 2010, I first had the inspiration to write this book. After living in Armenia for eight years, and knowing that change was in our future, we realized that we only had a few more months to enjoy everything we had grown to love so much. Armenia had become such a part of us, we couldn't let the details of that rich life be forgotten. I had to do something to both honor and preserve the story while allowing others to share in the adventure.

I began to write *I Am There* during our last few months in Armenia, continued during a one-year furlough in America, and completed the final pages during our first month in Estonia.

Real life often seems like a patchwork of unrelated events rather than an epic tale gracefully outlined, with every rough edge skillfully polished away. I am learning that we don't always know the significance of our struggles or the experiences we find along the paths of life until they can be viewed from the vantage point of time. This book is a collection of stories, pieced together in much the same way that they came to us.

If you will, walk with me for a while, while I attempt to bring to life a land and a people that deserve to be known. Allow yourself to pick up your baggage, walk out of a crumbling Soviet airport, and **be there**—a part of each story. I have no doubt that you, like me, will be changed by their lives and thankful for the journey.

Contents

Part One

I Am There

Chapter One

Where in the World?

I was 24 years old when I moved to Armenia. If I am honest, I didn't want to be there. The adventure of living in an obscure, developing nation and the life of a missionary felt like the cruel straps of a straitjacket.

Nothing about being a missionary was attractive to me. When churches and supporters showered praise for giving up all the wonderful things that I could achieve in America, I wondered if I was out of my mind. Truth be told, I wanted the American dream. I didn't long for the extravagant—just a 1920s home on a quiet street in a wonderful school district. Our weekends would be filled with pancake breakfasts in a quaint kitchen and family bike rides down tree-lined streets.

Don't misunderstand me, I loved missions trips. In my teen years we traveled to Belarus and Moscow, to South and Central America. I felt the overwhelming compassion of Christ as I visited special needs orphanages and held unbathed children or stayed in the ice-cold apartments of widowed babushkas living on miniscule pensions.

I felt a deep guilt for my lack of eagerness. When I looked into my husband Nick's eyes, I saw the passion and confidence every good missionary should possess. I was filled with the opposite. Fear. Worry. Disappointment.

But I found myself there.

In 2002, I sat in our director's office at our mission network's headquarters. I smiled at him, but deep down I was terrified of committing to a life of overseas service. His office window's drapes hung open to let the sun dance across his desk. I sort of found myself wishing the drapes had been drawn closed. That, at least, would have concealed my tight and nervous smile. I had even chosen a new red lipstick to wear on that day—the season's trendiest color. Why did I think that would help?

I can remember the director's deep, seasoned voice. I can recall the hopeful look in his eyes as he said, "What about going to Armenia? We've never had anyone work there before and we've been trying to get someone to go there for years."

Suddenly, I knew.

It was the early 1970s. They were hippies and living the dream of millions of listless youth disillusioned by the war and amped up by the music revolution.

She had brown hair, long and straight, and wore the fashion of rebellion —corduroy pants with a bell that showed earth toned, wooden heels, a brushed suede vest hung open over a bright purple silk blouse. The vest was worn open to reveal a copper-toned belt buckle that bore all the signs of the zodiac. She was a theater student at an elite, all women's college.

He had even longer hair and balanced atop high platform shoes, carried a tasseled leather purse he made himself, and drove a Cadillac hearse, even when it wasn't filled with oversized British sound equipment. The shock and irony of his transportation was a counter-culture bonus.

One night their worlds collided. He was playing guitar in a popular rock band, and she was the beauty in the crowd. Within a year, they were saying their marriage vows in the forest. She wore a wreath of flowers around her head and their Best Dog, a red, long-haired Irish Setter, laid on the minister's feet. He had a dream, and she abandoned her education to tour the country with the band in pursuit of a record deal.

The years that followed consisted of smoke-filled bars, communal living, and infested rentals where the band and their latest groupies would waste the night away with drugs and cheap love.

When the band broke up, the young couple settled in Kansas City, Missouri. It was while working a normal, reliable job at a trendy men's clothing store that he met a woman. They began as friends, but soon became more.

One day, he never came home. There were two place settings for a dinner that would never be eaten. A call and an emotionless voice that said, "I'm not coming home. I am moving in with her."

She was shocked. Devastated. Suddenly she was abandoned in a home and in a dream that had just died. The next morning dawned, and she was one figure, lying alone, in her double bed; curtains drawn, with no desire to move.

There is a moment in every person's life when we reach the limit of our resilience. The strength and self-assurance we possess to conquer the trials of our past are no longer sufficient for the crippling obstacle that confronts us. At that moment, we don't cry out for our wealth, or success or prized intellect to save us. The eyes of our soul open, and we see with clarity: there has to be something more. The happy, strong, generous and good in us feels thin. The soul calls out for the truth, and the tangibly real is given center stage.

She had grown up on a perfect street on the East coast. Her neighborhood was the one that young families would drive through and dream of saving up and buying a home in one day. It was a small island neighborhood on the Niagara River, quietly isolated from the upsurge of mid-century Niagara Falls. A little girl, Lucille, had moved in down the street, and the two were soon inseparable friends.

One friend grew up and followed her husband through the whirlwind life of a rock band; the other rode the hippie wave to Tucson where she met a man who had altered history by giving his life away. Lucille had become a lover of God and His revolutionary Son. Now working back in Niagara Falls, Lucille felt God leading her to quit her job and move to Kansas City. This was a crazy idea, but she obeyed.

As a young, single woman, Lucille packed up all of her belongings in her tiny car and began the long, two-day trek to Kansas City. She arrived on her best friend's doorstep and understood the mission she'd been given. Her best friend was rejected and alone.

Lucille invaded the thick atmosphere of hopelessness with love and truth. An elite education, a talented husband, and doting parents—she had tried to find her value in all of them. But now her heart laid torn open, and nothing seemed to be able to fill the void.

Rather than eating dinner alone after a long day of work or spending her weekends lost in the endless paths of whys and what-ifs, she had Lucille. Lucille listened and challenged the bitterness with love. She fought off those feelings of unforgiveness while laughing with her childhood friend. Little time had passed before Lucille had tracked down a life-giving church and introduced Leslie to the promises of the Bible. Lucille helped her find hope and life in Jesus Christ. She dedicated her life to God, and Lucille began to teach her the fundamentals of how to follow Him. In their naïve and simple faith, they began to pray that God would do a miracle.

A year passed.

Logic would say that hope was lost, but deep inside her, deeper and stronger than the dread and loneliness that filled her mind, was peace. She signed her name because he wanted her to. The divorce was finalized.

Not more than a week later, his thin figure slowly found its way up the steps and on to the porch of the home they once owned together.

A knock on a screen door. She barely recognized him. He was a shadow of the confident, mischievous man she knew. She eagerly swung open the frail door; he took one step towards her. He was stepping back into her life. The words escaped his lips with difficulty. But her confident peace put him at ease. They remarried and a baby girl was born nine months later as their first child. That little girl was me.

My mother's commitment to God continued, and she took me to church with her every week. My father had spent years mocking Christianity, but he could not deny the difference he sensed in his young wife. Although it didn't happen overnight, the depth of her love and peace had begun to wear down his skepticism. When I was four years old, my father laid on a couch, battling severe pneumonia, when he finally bowed his pride, whispered words of commitment and decided to follow Christ. His life was instantly and acutely changed.

Four years later, he said yes to filling in as the youth pastor, and what began as an experiment, turned into a life-long calling. For twenty years, his non-traditional history, quirky sense of humor and his ear splitting, guitar-driven worship brought thousands of teenagers through the church's doors.

Nineteen years later, in their mid-fifties, my parents embarked on a new adventure—reaching the youth of Europe. For the past decade, they have served as missionaries in The Netherlands.

Now as I sat in our mission director's office, I felt all of my fear and doubt melt away when he said that word.

Armenia.

See, Lucille, my mother's best friend who rearranged her entire life to walk my mother through the divorce and introduce my mother to Christ, is Armenian. Her family emigrated from Western Armenia and ended up buying the home right down the street from where my mother lived. My mom remembers this feisty Armenian family, their heated arguments, their passionate love for each other, and the food: stuffed grape leaves, rice pilaf and large amounts garlic that would eventually seep out of your pores.

From this Armenian culture came someone who was willing to listen to God's silent, strong voice and obey. Without her love, guidance, support and prayers, my parents would have most likely never remarried. I would have never been born.

"Will you go to Armenia?"

Peace. My body relaxed, my fake, tight smile became true. In that office, God was showing me that He knew my history, He knows my future, and He wanted to use me—the least likely, least willing person.

On June 16, 2003, I boarded a plane to Armenia. Twenty-seven hours later, I stepped off the plane, and I was there. As I made my way to baggage claim, I was overwhelmed by the sea of perfectly trimmed black hair, black leather jackets and black pointy dress shoes. I could barely squeeze my luggage through the small opening in the crowd. Cigarettes hung out of their mouths, flowers ready as they crowded and pushed each other to get a peek through the door. When their long-awaited friend or relative would finally appear, tired, unshaven faces would ignite with joy. Hugs and kisses were lavished on weary travelers.

No close family or long-lost friends anxiously awaited our arrival. We had left that all behind. I was in a place that I never expected to be, and our adventure began. I never dreamed I would be there. I never felt qualified to be there. And now as I write from America, I realize that a part of myself was left there—some of my immaturities and hurts, my selfish desires and dreams, sweat and silent prayers.

As I look back over those years in Armenia, there is one thing that sustained me and rang true. Jesus had chosen one last thing that he wanted to emphasize to his disciples. Out of everything he could have chosen to speak about on his final day, he chose these words.

"As you go, train everyone you meet, far and near, in this way of life, marking them by baptism in the threefold name: Father, Son, and Holy Spirit. Then instruct them in the practice of all I have commanded you. I'll be with you as you do this, day after day after day, right up to the end of the age." *(Matthew 28:19, The Message)*

Jesus promised he would be with us to the ends of the earth, and honestly, I felt like I was there. When I stepped off that airplane into that concrete Soviet airport, He was there. He had been working in Armenia, and He was there waiting to fulfill His promise to me—to be with me. Day after day—even to the very end of my life.

I was there, because He was there.

This book is a collection of some of my favorite experiences and stories from nearly a decade of our lives spent in Armenia. Armenia is a small forgotten country filled with amazing people. I had the opportunity to sit in their living rooms, sip countless cups of tea and hear their remarkable stories. Those stories deserve to be told, written and etched in ink on the pages of a book. I have the privilege to be their voice in places they will never walk.

I am there.

Chapter Two
The Story of the Missing Key

I have met many missionaries who have prepared their entire lives to move overseas—to share their lives, their food and hearts with a people who may or may not really care. They eagerly anticipate the moment when they receive their final approval to board an airliner, just a few suitcases in hand. They are cramped in their seats for 24 straight hours of travel, but they will endure anything to attain the dream of serving in a distant land.

During the process of raising our financial support, I must say I was pretty enthusiastic, too. I enjoyed speaking at churches and missions conventions. We were praised for our bravery, and the conversation always ended with the proverbial slap on the back, "Better you than me!"

Why me?

I didn't need God to answer. I *knew* my path ended up in Armenia. But, when it came down to the last few months before our eminent departure—in the middle of stuffing our suitcases with ibuprofen, anti-bacterial gel, cake mixes and the biggest bag of chocolate chips in the known world—I was anything but ready to go. I suddenly couldn't help feeling what young bachelors call "cold feet" on their wedding day.

Did I realize what I was committing to when I said yes to missions?

Did I really want to leave my family, work and life in America behind for this?

Let's face it, there's something nice about predictability. Predictability is safe and warm; it means you can go to the store to buy a bag of chocolate chips any time you want.

Was it really God who was asking me to live and work in Armenia?

But, if you know me well, you can probably discern how I was raised. I can still imagine my father standing across from me in the kitchen of our Victorian home with its blue gingham wallpaper and Formica countertops.

"Olivia. If you said that you would do something, you are going to do it and do it well until it's finished. You committed. That's it. No backing out."

OK, Dad. I boarded that plane for Armenia with a tinge of excitement and a hoard of fear. My heart probably beat 150 times a minute as the back wheels took off the tarmac, and America was long gone.

For me, those first few months in Armenia were tough. I remember sitting on our balcony, looking out over the entire city center—ugly Soviet apartment buildings; smog from old Russian cars; honking, honking, honking; old women climbing steps with bags full of produce from the outdoor market; young women making their way through broken sidewalks in stilettos.

I sat with my legs tucked up underneath me and thought, "What in the world am I doing here? I hate it here. I want to leave."

Later that day, I left our apartment to enter the hot sauna of Yerevan, stumbled over crooked sidewalks and entered a smoke-filled Internet club. I remember e-mailing my parents a rather succinct message, namely one word in all caps – "HELP!"

Poor Nick. This was everything my husband had dreamed about since he was 17. He had spent years studying missiology as preparation for this very day. He valeted cars at an upscale restaurant and substitute taught in the inner city classrooms of Minneapolis to make enough money to pay off his school loans. All of this was so we could pursue his big dream: missions.

Then he married me, a girl who couldn't last even four weeks.

Before we got engaged, Nick had expressed his desire to be a missionary. But amidst the sparkly new diamond ring and registering for new towels and linens, the reality of missions seemed to get lost in translation. Even when I did allow myself to visualize our life overseas, the scene was in a charming European café. The people would whisper polite pleases and thank yous, and "Yes, I will have another croissant." But this was a hot, dusty city where the drink of choice at cafés appeared to be vodka.

I remember one of these early days very well. During this part of our journey we were alone and just trying to survive in Armenia. We walked everywhere. It had been months and our apartment still wasn't settled. Language lessons revealed just how incredibly difficult the Armenian language is. Every day was spent fighting to learn how to locate the next thing on our list and we would accomplish a mere one, maybe two errands.

On this day we were walking home from the post office where we paid our utility bills. Who stands in line to manually pay utility bills, anyway? What happened to the concept that a slap of the stamp sends a payment on its way? In the building, sitting in a corner, was a huge bust of the head of Lenin. His eerie eyes seemed to follow me as I walked around. They appeared to say, "Move too far to the right, or too far to the left and I will break you."

As we returned home, I don't remember our exact discussion. Perhaps we were trying to decide the time of our language lessons, another scavenger hunt for a necessity, or whether or not to invite guests to our small apartment. Whatever it was, all of the fear of losing my identity in this country immediately surfaced. I was done fighting it. I had had enough. In Armenia, I felt like I had lost my freedom.

When I am at my emotional end, I shut down. I don't argue. I don't talk it through, but I resist being controlled with every cell of my being. I am stubborn. Nick is stubborn. We were both stressed in ways that we had never experienced. As Nick pried into my silence, I began to break. I teared up and looked away, hating everything and everyone that met my gaze. And then I heard something I didn't expect.

"Olivia, you are more important than anything to me. You're more important than missions or Armenia. God can use us anywhere. What if we give it six months? If at the end of that time you feel like you do today, then I will, without any shame, tell all of our supporters that we are returning home."

Wow. My Grandma was right when she said she KNEW that I had married a good man. The freedom Nick gave me helped my entrapped soul start to breathe a bit easier and to enjoy Armenia for what it was—difficult living arrangements and all.

Our apartment was housed in the old Composers' building, a four-story structure built to house the famous composers of Soviet Armenia. The center of the building looked like a version of the White House's veranda, but was crafted out of pink stone. It had pillars and large round balconies that opened into a concert and rehearsal hall and the official music guild offices. I loved going throughout our day, windows open, and letting the sounds of the best choirs in the nation flow through our windows.

We moved into the apartment with a promise that the renovations would be completed soon. But the workers didn't exactly share our urgent desire to have a nice kitchen to cook in, and missed numerous deadlines and installation appointments. It was really only the beginning of learning the art of being flexible. And just when we were beginning to relax into the unpredictable rhythm of Armenian life, our apartment's water was suddenly cut off. In an effort to adjust, we tried going for a few days without showers. The dishes began to pile up. Finally, after a week, a new American friend had mercy and invited us to her home for a wonderful meal and allowed us to finally wash off our daily grime in her shower.

Around 11 p.m. when my long hair was finally clean, but still wet, we left our friend's home and entered a taxi parked on a nearby street.

He safely delivered us in front of our building, and then putting his hand in his pocket to pull out our apartment door's key, Nick panicked. No key!

Now to give you the full picture, this key was huge. It was about four inches long and reminded me of some old Victorian key that you would picture sticking out of C.S. Lewis' wardrobe in a novel. It was a heavy, brass, weapon of a key, and it had somehow fallen out of Nick's pocket.

It was gone.

After calling our friend and surveying the ground, we realized that the key was back in the taxi. The only problem was, we didn't have the first clue on how to find the taxi. Yerevan was full of private citizens who turned their cars into taxis. Unfortunately, we hadn't called a taxi service but had seen him on the side of the road and naturally, we jumped in. There was absolutely no way of finding him. We were worn out, and all of the vehicles and drivers in this city of one million people looked basically the same to us.

That was it for me. No water. No key. No phone number for our landlord. It was now midnight. I sat down on the curb all slumped over. My first impulse was to run—not walk—back to that stifling hot Internet club and buy a return ticket home on the next morning's 4:00 a.m. flight. I was weak and exhausted.

Fortunately for us, however, Armenia, like New York City, is a late-night culture. Even at midnight, many of Yerevan's small shops were still open.

I sat down on a dirty curb right in front of a one room, family-owned convenience store. The store owner, a grandma, noticed my look of despair and immediately came to help me. I didn't understand her, but the look on my face must have broken the language barrier. I didn't know the word for "key" or "lost." Yet instinctively, she could just tell we had a problem. So she pulled us into her shop and through a back door, to a hidden entrance into her apartment.

"MOMENT. MOMENT." She kept using her very limited English repeatedly.

She picked up her old green circa 1970 Soviet rotary phone and called her granddaughter—a girl who'd studied some English.

"My grandma says that you look very sad, and she wants to know how to help."

So there I was, in a stranger's home, explaining our story. Handing the phone back to the grandma, I waited for the translation.

"NO PRO-BLEM. NO PRO-BLEM." She patted my shoulder and gave a reassuring smile. They offered us tea and snacks from her tiny store.

She then proceeded to call her son who soon arrived in his Russian Volga—the pride of Soviet era automobiles—happy to help. He drove Nick all around Yerevan looking for the taxicab as I stayed back with the grandma sipping tea and using hand gestures to communicate. Her son drove Nick back to the spot where we'd found the taxi. No luck. The other taxi drivers parked on the street recognized the cab Nick described and said that our driver would be back, in the same spot, on Monday. It was terrible news, considering it was two days later, but what could we do?

Only left with one option: return home and hope the door somehow remained unlocked or perhaps, out of sheer weariness from our constant complaining, would magically open. It was now 1 a.m., and the steel-sided door remained unmovable. Without any other brilliant ideas at our disposal, we decided to knock on our neighbors' door. This would be our first face-to-face introduction.

After hearing our story, suddenly the whole three-floor apartment building came alive, and we witnessed the Armenian community spring to action. Every member of every family came out of their apartment—bathrobes, slippers, jogging pants matched with sleeveless white undershirts, chest hair billowing. We were in one of those low-budget foreign language films, but we were caught on the other side of the screen and could not read the subtitles. Armenian and Russian words echoed off the concrete steps like bullets from a machine gun. Hands and arms flew, reinforcing emotion. They were all trying to help these poor naïve Americans get back inside their home.

We knew that Armenians are known for their hospitality, but this was our initiation. As the coffee, tea, cookies, candy and fruit made their way around the group, we realized that we were experiencing something we would never forget. Through our very limited Armenian that night, and their limited English, we became friends. We became a part of our community.

Finally, one of them motioned for silence. She had tracked down, through who knows how many degrees of separation, our landlady's cell phone number. They found her. She was on her way with the second key at 1 a.m. A sigh of relief calmed the atmosphere and smiles were exchanged

Our landlady, we found out, is quite famous in Yerevan. She is a stage actress with a deep smoky voice. She arrived in leopard print and stiletto heels. The film metaphor was complete.

I suddenly realized that we hadn't moved to a hostile culture that was waiting to eat and destroy us. Rather, we had moved to Yerevan, a large capital city that was more like a generous family who was always willing to help anyone in need.

True, they may nearly run you over when you're crossing the street. But when it comes to truly helping someone in need, the Armenians always came through.

I suddenly felt safe in the hands of these people, and something changed in me that day. We delivered flowers to the grandmotherly store owner and began to chat and have tea with our neighbors.

Six months came and went, and I found myself falling in love with the people and longing to do anything I could to help serve them. Our eight years in Armenia have been the greatest adventure of our lives thus far. And, it all started with a lost key.

Interestingly enough, keys are usually designed to lock up treasures; to keep secrets safe. Until that day, I had been walking the streets of Yerevan with my emotions guarded and my heart locked shut. But the recovery of our antique key finally unlocked a piece of my spirit and I finally felt ready to learn and explore the streets of Yerevan—but not in high heels!

Chapter Three
Surviving Firsts

Upon our arrival in Armenia, we began to unwind a long string of Armenian firsts. It was our first time to live outside of America. We walked daily to language lessons and forced our brain to comprehend complex grammar, strange sounds, and an ancient alphabet. While trying to verbally practice some words, some Armenians would patiently strain to listen while others would just shake their heads and walk on.

My first day in Armenia, I was escorted to a large open-air market filled with the chatter of Armenians bartering the prices of fruit and vegetables for their next meal. My guides were seasoned missionaries, now my dear friends, Pat Beiler and Eloise Neely. They had flown to Armenia for the sole purpose of helping us find a home and navigate the first week of life in a new world.

Pat's smile gleamed with excitement as she explained that this is where I would learn to love to shop. The vibrant colors caught my eye immediately. The sellers would constantly polish and spritz their fruit and vegetables arranged in to a perfect pyramid. Day after day, I wanted to bite into one of the sumptuous apricots that the Armenian nation is known for. Their pale orange skin covered with fuzz looked so flavorful, but then I remembered travelers' rule number one: don't eat local produce washed in city water until your body has acclimated to the local germ population. Wistfully, I walked on.

I then walked by the butchers' stands, and a wave of repulsion swept over me. A stream of blood flowed from the butcher's block to the curb. Piles of pigs' feet baked on a table in the sun. Cut meat was hanging from hooks above the butcher's head attracting a plethora of flies. My visit to the city market was the first of many times that I felt quite overwhelmed. But, everywhere we went, there was one important "first" that we had not experienced. In the unwritten book, *Armenian Necessary Steps to Adulthood*, it states that you must have a child within your first year of marriage.

How could we tell them we had chosen not to have a child and spend the first five years of married life as a couple before adding to our family? We had finished college, paid off our debt and moved overseas. We were trying to learn the language and adjust to a new culture. Simple tasks such as banking, shopping and driving in a sea of cars that often ignored traffic lights, thoroughly exhausted us. How could we add the demands of a baby to all of this? We soon learned that there was something in our plan that was completely baffling to the Armenian psyche.

Pastors would ask us. People in the church would question. Neighbors would inquire. Grocery Store clerks would pry.

"Do you have kids?"

Our answer was always, "No."

Their reply was always, "Oh…you must be newlyweds."

"No, we've been married for five years."

Then came the cultural clash, the confused look, and the subtle pat on my flat belly. "I will pray for you to be healed so you can have children."

The unwritten rulebook says that marriage equals a baby. There is no other way; no questions asked. To choose any other way is culturally unimaginable. It's part of an Armenian woman's DNA—to bear beautiful dark-haired, brown-eyed Armenian children. And to be unable to have a child is one of the greatest burdens a woman can bear.

During our first year in Armenia, we visited as many churches as we could. We wanted to meet all the pastors and their congregations. As we did this, I had, without even trying, recruited an army of moms and grandmas who were praying for me to conceive my first child. In their hearts and prayers, they wanted joy for me and the promise of a future. I, on the other hand, was sticking to our original plan. No baby yet.

Perhaps a culture's values can seep into your life just by drinking their water, eating their food, breathing their air. Or, perhaps God has learned to truly listen to the Armenian women who have endured so much. I found myself, without even trying, expecting our first child after only a year in Armenia.

I was completely surprised when I found out that I was already eight weeks pregnant with not one child, but two. Twins! The ultrasound showed, however, that one child was significantly smaller than the other. My pregnancy was at risk. The doctor put me on bed rest for the next four weeks of my first trimester to preserve both lives inside of me.

The following Sunday, Nick was scheduled to speak at a church three hours away in the village of Jermuk. I, following the doctor's orders, stayed at home in our warm Yerevan apartment.

Nick showed up a few minutes before the church service began to an apartment that the pastor had converted into a church. The room was packed with chairs and people. The walls vibrated with loud worship music. After Nick's sermon, and praying for nearly everyone in the room, he was approached by a woman in her 60s.

"I didn't sleep at all last night. God kept repeatedly waking me up and showing me an image of you and your wife. I have never seen you before, but you were definitely the one in my dream! He gave me very specific instructions to pray for you in the same way that I pray for my daughter. My daughter has been pregnant many times and has miscarried every baby. I pray for her so deeply. God wanted me to pray for your wife and your baby with the same love and fervency I pray for my future grandchild."

This woman did not know our story. She did not know the reason that I had stayed home from the long journey to Jermuk. But, God had awakened someone to pray, with the anguish of a desperate Armenian grandmother, on our behalf.

Four weeks later, I returned to the doctor and one baby remained. The first months of my pregnancy went well with no morning sickness and very little weight gain. My Armenian doctor said the pregnancy was perfect, and I even considered having my baby in Armenia. A Canadian couple we knew had recently had a baby girl there without any problems. I felt a subtle pressure to have our baby there too. I did not want to hurt the feelings of our new friends who had prayed for us so diligently. We wanted to show them we loved them and trusted their country with our whole hearts.

But after praying and talking with our family, we eventually decided to return home to America for the birth. Before we knew it, those six months flew by, and I was on an airplane headed home.

I remember how excited I felt to meet the doctor that would deliver our baby boy, Oliver, in America. I walked into the office with my cute six-month belly, and I couldn't wait to hear how wonderful the pregnancy was progressing. But that was not the news I received.

On that day, we discovered that Oliver was fighting for his life. He was diagnosed with IUGR (Intra-Uterine Growth Restriction). For some reason, his body was not getting what it needed to grow. It had delayed the growth of every part of his body, but was putting all of its energy into preserving the development of his control center, the brain.

Suddenly I realized that Oliver was starving inside of me, and the Armenian doctor, with her limited resources, had never diagnosed his condition. It was then that I breathed a silent prayer of thankfulness that I had returned home.

My last three months of pregnancy were filled with weekly tests, high-level ultrasounds and consults with top doctors at the Children's Hospital. On the morning of March 8, 2005, I sat in the living room of a beautiful Minnesota lake home that a family had let us live in for the pregnancy. It was one of those dreamy, crisp Minnesota winter days that draws you inside to a comfortable chair and good movie. But our doctor's appointment forced us out into the weather.

On the ultrasound screen they measured Oliver's head size and the length of his legs. The monitor held to my belly with an elastic strap amplified the sounds of the womb. The technician went through her routine and we listened to the swishing. She jiggled my belly, changed my position and gave me a sugary drink. "Let's see if the sugar will wake him up."

No response. The technician left the room and returned with my doctor. "It's time to take him out. Go home and get your things. You'll be a mom this time tomorrow."

On a cold, winter afternoon in Minneapolis, our dear Oliver David Puccini was born. He cried out his dramatic, pitiful cry. We could see the outlines of his rib bones and joints. But his low point had passed, he had been delivered to us. He was alive and well, and after two days in the hospital, was allowed to come home.

Oliver was starving and drank twice the normal amount of milk, and he gained weight twice as fast. He was a sweet and calm baby with a crinkly forehead and large, beautiful eyes that he would eventually grow into. We returned to Armenia when Oliver was just two months old, and he continued to flourish. He developed quite the tummy under the love of all the Armenians and the protection of His God.

We almost lost Oliver, and if I had stayed in Armenia for his birth, he would have most likely been stillborn. But God, from the time he was born, held Oliver in His hands.

Oliver was born small, and in the midst of moving between countries and cultures, may feel overlooked. But we know that God recognized him enough to awaken an old woman in a forgotten Armenian village to pray for his survival. Often, when I tousle Oliver's long brown hair or look into his deep green eyes, I am reminded of the promise that God is with us. God can fight for us—even when we are weak and helpless.

When we live in view of this truth, we realize that we were created to love, to dream, and to live with the absolute knowledge that ultimately, God, the creator of the universe, has our back.

"Before I shaped you in the womb,
I knew all about you.
Before you saw the light of day,
I had plans for you."
— Jeremiah 1:5, The Message

Chapter Four

God is in the Details

It was bone-chilling cold that day. The frigid mountain air had moved down to Yerevan and hovered like a giant puff of smoke over the city. I thought about our Armenian friends, many of them did not have central heating in their homes. Most trees in the city had been cut down, years before, as firewood. Books too had gone up in flames on such a day as this. But me? I was hot. I mean sweaty, dripping hot.

Six miles an hour at an incline of 25 percent, the treadmill was set and my feet were diligently pounding the moving belt beneath me. My headphones were plugged in, and CNN International was playing on the built-in TV screen, allowing me to be perfectly distracted while exercising.

I gazed through the glass panels in front of me and struggled to find Oliver swimming in the large Olympic size pool below. A wall of windows that allowed Armenia's sunny disposition to shine through illuminated the newly renovated pool. On the other side of these windows stood modern stone mansions encased in elaborate ironwork amidst old, crumbling Soviet-style concrete apartment complexes.

I inhaled and exhaled. Nothing was more mundane than running indoors. For some reason, I was routinely driven to exercise. Well, I know the reason. The eating disorder that gripped me in high school was always knocking at the door. But when I exercised and ate healthfully, the struggles that came with the disease were kept at bay. Suddenly I found myself overwhelmed with the dichotomy of my situation.

Years ago, I had given up all the comforts of America. We sold the few possessions we had accumulated through our first five years of marriage and packed our entire lives into a few suitcases. I had been willing to give it all up, even if some days it was more reluctantly. With an unwilling heart, I asked God to change me. With my heart beating quickly as I ran up the incline, I realized He had.

When I ran on that treadmill that day on the second floor of Armenia's new Gold's Gym International, I was overwhelmed with gratitude. I felt as if God had built that gym just for me. Yes, even at the risk of sounding selfish, for me. Of course, deep down I knew it was not solely built for my use and pleasure. But why would Yerevan with its freezing homes, cratered streets and prolific beggars have a gym better than most of the more important cities of the former Soviet Unions? Well, the answer is this: God is in the details.

God's amazing provision did not end when I walked out the doors of the gym. We found a beautiful duplex that looked and felt like an American home. It was invitingly warm and when friends ate around our table, hours would pass as we conversed, and I knew they felt comfortable. Never mind the occasional four-inch long poisonous camel spiders found hiding in the toe of my shoe. I loved it.

After four years in Armenia, I felt like I was being consumed by the mission and no longer had any expression that was purely my own. Within a few weeks of verbalizing my frustration, through tears, to Nick, I was offered a position as a group cycling teacher and relished every opportunity to meet new people as we sweat together and mounted the hills of life in Armenia as a team.

Our ability to have a second child should have been easy. We already had our wonderful son, Oliver. So to us, another baby was not a question of if but when. After one year of trying, frustration began to set in. Fertility testing had confirmed that I had a problem, and I prepared myself to let another dream go. After all, I already had one child while many couples long for just one and can't conceive any.

A friend told me about a fertility doctor in Yerevan, so I made an appointment, but inside I was certain my visit would only provide a prescription for an older, recalled drug. To my surprise, I found a Europe-educated Armenian fertility doctor and under his care, we were able to have Ava—a true gift from God—at a fraction of the *impossible* American price for the same treatment.

During our eight years in Armenia, God took care of every important and minute detail. To think I was willing to give these unforeseen blessings up during our first months there shamed me. I was ready to give it all up, and once I did, God gave me so much more.

Now that I have returned to America for a year after eight years of living overseas, I find my willingness to sacrifice has waned. With each month that passes on my home soil, I find myself clinging to any remnant of the American dream that remained, embedded, in my soul. Can I once again step on that plane and leave everything behind and have a trust that God will provide for every need and every detail? Our furniture is sitting, packed up in our home in Armenia. We've been asked to fulfill a new mission and lead a church planting team to the least religious nation in our area, Estonia. That perceived threat to my foundation of security is felt once again. The comfort I experienced in Armenia started to create invisible cracks in my true ability to sacrifice. Now, I am called once again.

Walking through American malls, I find myself struggling with our next missionary assignment. Estonia has few hours of sunlight in the winter, and the people appear to be less friendly than Armenians. A chai tea at Starbucks, a sale at Gap Kids, and a quick run through Target are pleasures taken for granted now. And I am trying my hardest not to consume my precious luggage space with yet another big bag of chocolate chips. But in the end, I will stuff my allotted number of suitcases to the brim with everything that America can provide.

I find myself thinking that if we are well-funded, find the perfect home, and if I can squeeze a sun lamp into my carry-on to help brighten the dark winters, then maybe I will dare to go and live overseas again.

Every Sunday we speak in a different church to raise our support for our ministry goals in Estonia. We have seen the generosity of churches across the nation who are willing to give so we can go and establish a church. But, our year back in America is like a roller coaster that mounts the great hills and then plummets in the midst of exhaustion and doubts. In those moments, God reminds us that we are not self-sufficient. We can look back on our recent days in Armenia and have absolute confidence that He will provide for every need.

"Remember," He says softly. "I am in the details."

It's time to step on a plane with a few suitcases and take our dreams and our children across the world on a new adventure. As I sprint ahead, I try to hold on; my knuckles are white as I make a choice to pry my fingers from the safety handle one by one.

He built a gym for me in Armenia. I guess I can just let go, keep on running, and enjoy the ride.

Part Two
I am Changed

Chapter Five

The Doctor is in: No Appointment Required?

It was a hot August morning in 2003. We had only been in Armenia a few months when we hosted our first missions team from America. They had traveled halfway across the world to serve the churches there. That morning we dragged our bodies out of bed and arrived early to make sure all the logistics were in place—did they eat enough of the breakfast of meat, cheese and bread to endure the day? Did the small white vans we hired to transport them arrive on time? Was some poor soul forced to stay back because he had lost the battle to some new, exotic food?

We stood on the burgundy granite steps outside the hotel, chatting with the team and attempting to resist the many peddlers vying for our attention. Suddenly, sirens drowned out our conversation. A white ambulance, flashing red and yellow lights, sped up to the front door. A crew of what looked like 1950s era TV nurses, wearing white from head to toe complete with tiny white triangular caps pinned in their hair, dashed from the ambulance and ran inside.

A few minutes later, the ambulance driver re-emerged out the front door, and raced back to the ambulance. The motor started, the ambulance lurched backwards into traffic, shifted into first gear, sirens and lights blaring, and rushed off without a patient. Five minutes passed, his ambulance sped around the corner again and screeched to a halt, one wheel fully on the curb. We gawked as he flung open the back doors and pulled out the defibrillator. As he ran toward the front door, his arms full of equipment, he tripped, crashing headlong into the lobby of the hotel. With his jaw clenched, he quickly gathered each piece and disappeared up the stairwell. We all stood there in amazement and were left to wonder what we had just witnessed.

After returning later from a full day of ministry, the front desk confirmed our suspicions. A guest had died in her room that morning. She was an American Armenian visiting her family's homeland. She was gone. I imagined how her grown children would've reacted if they'd been there to see an ambulance arrive unprepared— their mother's life lost as a result.

After a few years of living in Armenia, there were many things that I grew to love and accept. I loved their hospitality with their open door, everything-I-have-is-yours mentality. I learned to accept their crazy driving; the take-your-foot-off- the-brake-when- you-leave and put-your-foot-on-the-brake-when-you-get-to-where-you're-going maneuvers. I waited for a crowd to gather around Ava in the supermarkets, as they kissed her hands and took pictures of her blonde hair and chubby cheeks with their cell phones. But, when one of us would become ill, I knew I was about to experience one of my greatest cross-cultural challenges—an encounter with the post-Soviet medical system the Armenians inherited.

There were many brilliant Armenian doctors and scientists who were forced to practice with outdated medical equipment while doing their best in a system that had been designed under Soviet corruption. And sometimes finding these world-class specialists in a complicated medical system proved to be an overwhelming quest for this naïve American.

Our language study had begun, and we were earnest students. We wanted to communicate with all the new people we were meeting. So every day we would wake up, gather our things and begin the journey to our lesson. Like kids, we would stop at a corner convenience store about the size of a telephone booth, and purchase a bag of pretzels and juice box for our day.

It was July and now very hot in Yerevan. Our new vehicle sat parked in a garage as we waited months for its registration to finalize. The first few weeks, we would run down the four flights of stairs behind our apartment building and hail any taxi that would stop on the busy street below.

Our language skills were so limited that we would show the driver a well-worn piece of paper with our school's address written in Armenian letters. We had no way of knowing if he recognized the address until we either safely arrived or watched the minutes pass as he attempted to find his way. As we sat on a scratchy piece of Oriental rug that served as a seat protector, we looked out the open windows, observing our foreign surroundings and the people who inhabited it as we drove by.

Our luxurious rides in old Russian-made taxis, with no air conditioning, abruptly ended when we finally realized that we were paying ten times the going rate for each ride. Our lack of language skills, our clothing, Nick's height and blue eyes, the overwhelmed look in our eyes—they were all dead giveaways. Basically, we were foreigners who could be taken advantage of. I guess taxi drivers are the same breed the world over.

Eventually, we were forced to change our routine and make our morning commute like the majority of Armenians. Once outside our door, we would walk for blocks to a Soviet-style, underground subway. The old escalators would creak as they frenetically descended at a sharp incline. The platforms and walls were covered with cold, brown stone that created an ominous, austere space. A wall of crisp air would wash down the platform twirling discarded trash around our feet, and suddenly the room would echo with the sound of screeching wheels. The doors flew open with a shudder and passengers pushed their way on and off the car. A sweaty ride filled with hot people and another twenty-minute walk to the university became a daily adventure.

One morning as we walked to class, it felt like the sun's rays were piercing my skin like needles. Already grouchy and missing our cab with the *Aladdin*-esque carpet seat covers, I realized I had a big problem. Red spots with a tiny blister had erupted all over my stomach and back. Sizzling with pain, I made a decision that I'd skip the trip to the doctor's office.

Sadly, the pain grew, and the spots weren't going away. Turns out, I had shingles— the chicken pox virus that resurfaces in adults during times of high stress. Despite my best efforts to recover on my own, my language teacher finally dragged me to see the university's nurse who quickly diagnosed my problem and told me where I could track down the proper medication (without a prescription). Considering how rotten I felt, I looked at her with eyes of anticipation; waiting for her to say I had eaten too much immune-compromising cold ice cream under the Armenian sun or perhaps, it was the windy draft in the subway stations that had penetrated my skin and caused the shingles.

The medical system we encountered was so different from our own. When our colleague had to have emergency surgery for appendicitis, she was shocked when they rolled her into the operating room with her street clothes on and performed surgery. Even stranger, when awakened, she was still wearing the same clothing she had on when she showed up. During her hospital stay, our Armenian friends took on the role of her family— providing all care, supervision, meals and financial gifts for the nursing staff—not exactly how we roll in the United States.

One of the most difficult things for me to do while in Armenia was to take our children to the pediatrician's office. I had mastered the art of shopping in open-air markets and driving like an Armenian, but my trips to the doctor's office with my sick children became one of my most overwhelming tasks. The Armenians had a system that worked for them, but it would paralyze me as I stood frozen by the chaos in the halls of the clinic. There were no actual appointments, just a blue and white plaque posted outside the door etched with the pediatrician's hours. I would come, carrying my sick baby on my hip, and wade into the mass of moms carrying their own sick children outside the office door. With no waiting room or benches to sit on, we all just stood there. And waited. And waited some more. Kids coughed. And cried. They sneezed, and we all were miserable.

After waiting for what felt like eternity, an acquaintance of the doctor would show up, knock on the door, and be given immediate access—passing us all up in line. The Armenians were accustomed to this *system,* but I stood there with my screaming child, and with puppy-dog eyes, hoping the doctor would have mercy on me and remember where my spot was in the line. But I quickly learned that the line really didn't really matter. Instead, the victors were the most aggressive, the ones who "proved" their child was the sickest and who managed to get their foot in the door first when it cracked open. I hated every moment of it.

Once inside the doctor's office, those subtle details that we accept as universal health code were thoroughly violated. The doctor, without washing her hands, would sit my child down on an examination table that hadn't been cleaned or disinfected, no butcher paper to protect my baby from any germs left living. Then I waited for the diagnosis and the undeniable clicking of the Armenian tongue as she compared the size of my children to the size of the small Armenian children surrounding them. They were always too fat, too weak and their heads were definitely way too big. The doctor would then prescribe the necessary medication and follow up with an order to switch my children to an all-vegetable diet to reduce the size of their bellies. Needless to say, that was hardly the encouragement a tired mother needed after hours and hours of waiting in line.

I was in Yerevan, the veritable New York City of Armenia! I had access to the nation's best hospitals and the best doctors whenever I was in need. If you can imagine what my experience was like in the nation's capital, imagine the climate of the hospitals and medical system in the small towns and villages.

Some of the greatest snapshots I have of Armenia in my mind came from the free medical clinics we had the opportunity of organizing and hosting. The clinics were held in one of the most desolate areas of Armenia—in the Yezdi Kurdish villages of the mountains. Some of these villages were so isolated, due to large amounts of snow in the winter months, that if a woman went into labor, she would be pulled by a horse or snowmobile for more than an hour to the nearest clinic.

Our doctors and nurses from Chicago and Denver were forced to sit in a small minivan that leaned to one side as it passed over huge potholes and jolted each one of them out of their jetlag. The road to the Kurdish villages was among the worst in Armenia— with holes so large they would cover the width of the entire road and the only way to avoid losing an axle was to drive in the grassy fields on the shoulder.

Our goal was not only to host medical clinics, but also to raise the position of Pastor Baris and his church of Kurdish Christians in the region. The clinics were held on the second floor of his church building, and it brought nearly every single person in the community through his doors to receive treatment.

Our naïveté was in full force the first day. We thought that people would show up in a steady stream throughout the day and patiently wait for their turn. We were greeted by a crowd of desperate people already waiting for some good (and free) Western medical advice. Women were holding crying children and old ladies stood in the corner with their heads covered, supported by walking canes.

Once our American doctors were set up in their assigned rooms, the clinic opened. Naturally, mayhem ensued. One person would be seen by a doctor, and then the sea of people would wait next to the door for an opportunity to rush in. Fighting to get in any way they could manage, they pleaded their case like a lawyer. They objected to waiting, pure and simple.

Our doctors worked to show the love of Christ in a tangible way. They listened patiently. They performed certain exams that none of us would want to give—especially on people who had not showered in days. They prayed with those whose ailments arose from deep emotional pain, and they cried for those that they were unable help.

But what none of us could handle was the chaos that filled the hallways! We put our heads together and a proper, pragmatic system was quickly devised. The following day, each patient was forced to register their names on a schedule and they were given numbers. Once that number was called, it was their turn to the see the doctor. It was a simple plan that was bound to work!

While it definitely led to less visible chaos, the numbers did not take into account thousands of years of Kurdish culture that had survived the threat of occupying empires, war, famine and endless winters. Numbers didn't determine social status or the level of desperation of a mother whose child's tongue prevented him from swallowing. Nor could they palliate the unyielding pain of an elderly woman who carried 60 pounds of water over three miles every day of her life. A number doesn't reduce the social status of a village elder, or the pecking order of religious hierarchy among Kurds.

There were the anxious mothers who held their crying children on their hips, number in hand, who had to get back to their villages to water the cattle, make a meal, clean the house, and serve a roomful of guests.

"Could you just see me now? The last bus to my village is leaving soon!"

And then there were the barterers, those who would approach someone with a better number and negotiate for a trade.

Needless to say, it was a wonderful—albeit stressful—experience. I saw elderly people finally receive some sound medical advice. I saw children with lazy, crooked eyes given a simple eye patch that, if used diligently, would solve their child's eye problem and give her the chance to walk throughout life with normal vision. I saw some with problems so great, we all wished we could fly them to be seen by one of the top specialists in the world—that was the kind of miracle they needed.

Pastor Baris had given everything to serve his Kurdish community, and these doctors sacrificed greatly to stand beside him, serve the Kurdish people, and their healing God.

We board a plane and travel halfway around the world to get a taste of the everyday challenges many accept as normal. We return home and suddenly the long drive-through line at Starbucks is no longer such an inconvenience. The twenty-minute wait at our wonderful doctor's office is a worthy delay for her excellent advice. We wish we could somehow sweep just a bit of our prosperity across the ocean to land on the front porch of an old Kurdish grandma. As we go to make a difference, we are changed.

I am changed.

"Jesus heard about it and spoke up, 'Who needs a doctor: the healthy or the sick? I'm here inviting outsiders, not insiders—an invitation to a changed life, changed inside and out.'"
—Luke 5:31–32, The Message

Chapter Six

A Celebration of Forgotten Women

I remember standing on a stage in one of the old cultural theaters the Soviets had erected in nearly every city and town during their occupation. The tall windows were covered by faded red velvet curtains, unevenly hung, tattered edges covered in dust.

The floor was covered by parquet wood in a decorative zigzag pattern, now worn, scratched and beyond repair. The wood chairs nearby had withstood years of use; repairs ceased at some point in the distant past. I remember the thunder as the seats would spring closed whenever the crowd would stand.

The hot July air hung stale as the theater filled with women. There were grandmothers who struggled up endless steps to the entrance. The room was also filled with young mothers, some with small children. Others had convinced their husbands to be babysitters for just one night so they could enjoy a few hours of freedom.

I admired them: hair straightened, beautiful sleeveless tops, carefully applied make-up and accessories. I gazed out upon this sea of women—a sea of black hair with the occasional brave soul who dyed her tresses blonde or burgundy red. I saw a wave of beauty, and then I looked over at the pastor's wife, Tsogher. She stood near the entrance and was one of the most beautiful women in the room with her large, standout eyes and high cheekbones that were graced with faint freckles. Tsogher radiated with joy as she watched each woman enter through the theater's doors.

This was her church. This was her group of women that she and her husband, Karen, had faithfully ministered to over the past decade of their lives.

"We all have a story, " I said, greeting them from the stage. "A distinct purpose to fulfill. Each one of us has a unique beauty that is meant to be shared."

Many of their eyes brightened as they realized their true value. Even in the midst of crushing circumstances and unspeakable tragedies, the strong arms of their heavenly Father await them. We spoke of God's intense love for them and His knowledge of every personal dream.

My words were simple and probably expected. There was no profound sermon or teaching; just a simple reminder of a basic, life-giving truth we often forget amidst the mundane responsibilities of life.

Nonetheless, the room filled with a permeable sense of peace and love. I looked into the audience and saw tears flowing from very weary eyes. In the corner, near the door, stood Tsogher and I watched as her petite hand wiped away some tears.

To this day, that moment is one the most vivid memories I have of my time in Armenia. If I left America just for that moment, then it was worth it all. Hope infused their burdened hearts that day and it was tangible.

The next four years brought many opportunities to help a church remind its community of women of God's purpose, peace and love. Through music, dancing, drama, and unabashedly pink decorations, we brought a message of God's hope for their lives.

At the conclusion of every evening, I loved looking out from the stage and seeing dozens of women being prayed for. When these women stepped out of their seats, came forward, and closed their eyes, many would turn their palms up to God as a sign that they were waiting for something from Him. They knocked at His door, and He came running to meet them. They would cry as the strain of their daily lives in Armenia was lifted off of their shoulders and replaced with a peace that was clearly recognizable on their worn faces.

After prayer, many of them would move to the church's foyer, chat with friends and sink their teeth in to elaborately carved fruit platters accompanied by diamond-cut baklava, dripping in honey—basically every Middle Eastern woman's dream!

These women's events were done in Armenia's largest cities and some of its most famous villages. As word of these events spread, the meeting halls were packed to capacity with women. If life in Armenia was challenging in the big cities, it was truly difficult in the villages. Many women would walk a mile up uneven, dusty roads for a chance to come and be a part of something designed especially for them.

Every person, even an American living in Armenia, dreams of being successful. Some days I would find myself, sitting at my desk and imagining what I would be capable of doing in America. Perhaps I could work and provide a future for my kids and have them grow up without the constant burden of that toy, that activity, that vacation, that college just being too expensive? This has been my greatest personal challenge in missions.

The opportunity to stand on a church's stage and see a room filled to the brim with hand-made decorations and 120 village women forever changed my perspective. How could I give up my once-in-a-lifetime opportunity to help this church's women, clad in black skirts and crisp white blouses, serve desserts baked in dozens of ovens, in countless kitchens throughout the village? How can I value the blessings God has given me without having witnessed an Armenian woman's external shell of weariness melt away and, if only for one hour, be reminded that God sees her in a forgotten home? He knows her dreams and struggles. He embraces them with His love and hope.

As I write this, I am in America, if only for one year. I live in a lovely house and I love to look at the beautiful, old trees that stand outside my office window. And then IT hits me.

IT is the reality that all these things I take for granted, as owed to me, are not enjoyed by many women in Armenia. Then I think there may be one who is sitting by her window looking to a treeless sky, remembering the day she was made to feel special and she knew God loved her beyond measure.

Chapter Seven
Changing Perspectives

{Written in Tbilisi, Georgia}

Mornings are my favorite time of day. The world awakes from the still of night, and the noisy hum of Yerevan is not yet full speed. I poke around the kitchen cabinet for my favorite cereal. This typical morning I was not sure if I was filled with worry or anticipation. A few hours later, we were leaving Yerevan to travel the narrow, windy mountain road that led north to the Republic of Georgia.

We forded lakes of fog that blanketed the high passes, and pleaded stubborn livestock to share the asphalt. My eyes traced the horizon as it leaped and dived with the outline of the mountains all around us. We reached what would be the highest elevation of our journey. I looked out to the left, and saw the house in which I stood just last week as a part of one of our medical outreaches. It is a simple home made of large, rose-colored volcanic stone—each porous block separated from the next by a thick layer of white mortar. The exterior was a puzzle of windows, doors and a modest roof.

I remember stepping out of the car and being greeted by the family's grandmother—the queen bee of the household. Chickens and turkeys shuffled to get out of our way as we stepped into the home. She kissed me on my cheek, and ushered us inside to a group of women waiting to hear Dr. Naomi's community health teaching.

We were still waiting for some women to free themselves from their daily chores at home and arrive for the training. As we were waiting, the doctor began to listen to each woman's personal issues and give them medical advice.

The bride of the home (the young daughter-in-law) had caught my attention. She was beautiful with light hazel eyes and chestnut brown hair. She was my age, but the burdens of village life made her look nearly ten years older. When I looked at her, I saw intelligence and determination in her eyes. She was the engine of the house, and nothing went on that she did not notice.

I saw her bring her timid eight-year-old son into the room. As they sat down adjacent to the doctor, I noticed the boy's eyes were like his mother's, and at first I perceived him to be a normal, active boy. But, the drool running out of his mouth and awkward tongue movements revealed a challenging problem: he could not speak.

It was obvious that his mind was sharp, but he could not control his tongue. He simply did not have a voice. I felt like I was looking at a person trapped by his body. His mind knew the language, but his tongue would not cooperate. Instead of crying out his mother's name in the middle of night, he was forced to just groan his need for help.

With weary words, the mother explained how she had done everything in her limited means to help her son. She'd taken him to doctors, had a procedure done that "untied" his tongue, and took him to a speech therapist. All of this was done with very little means and took great sacrifice. She asked for advice, and she asked for God to do a miracle.

At that moment, it was more than I could bear. Everyone in the room was staring at me as tears began to quietly flow.

Dr. Naomi, whose back was turned to me, said, "It seems like you've done everything possible. Olivia has had similar issues with her son, and I'd like to ask her to pray for you."

Similar issues? I knew it was true, but at the same time, I could not compare my story to this woman's who had endured so much more.

Yes, I also have a son who, during his early years, had developmental and speech delays.

Yes, I also have a son that I believe is very smart, but has had people judge him because he can't grip a pencil correctly or speak with clarity and fluency expected of him.

Yes, I've tried everything within my means to help him and my means have fallen short. I've lived a life overseas in a country that does not have English speech therapists or occupational therapists.

Yes, I, like this mother, love him more than anything and pray to God that He will lighten my son's burden and heal his body so that he can truly express himself with ease and confidence.

But, I am not like this mother. My son can talk.

Suddenly, I felt as if the five years of worry and pain I have felt during my journey with Oliver were being multiplied one hundred times as I watched this woman's simple repetitive action of taking a napkin and wiping the drool from her mute son's mouth.

I stood up and I prayed with all the faith I had within me. I firmly declared that God had given this boy a voice, even if it was never heard. I asked God to reach His healing hand into this boy's body and perform a miracle. I affirmed the love of the mother and reassured her that God had heard her cries and had seen everything she had done for her son. I pleaded with God to work on this boy's behalf.

Heal him. Help his body give wings to his voice.

If living overseas has taught me anything, it has taught me perspective. Life, at its core, is all about perspective. My son struggles to hold a pen correctly, tie his shoes, sometimes stutters and has words that are incomprehensible.

This woman is holding on and waiting for her eight year old son to cry out one single word. I realize that I am privileged to feel just a little of the pain she is feeling. And, because of that pain, my prayer arises from somewhere deeper and more primal than the intellect.

I am reminded of what a great privilege it is to live in Armenia and realize that I am a part of a greater sisterhood. True, I may be giving up the friendship of my American friends who meet and sip coffee weekly as their kids play, I really miss that. But, in exchange, God has allowed me to be part of an international circle of women—rich and poor, loved and rejected, hopeful and hopeless. And, once again, over and over, I am reminded that we are more alike than we could ever imagine.

You can strip everything away from me and place me in a Kurdish village. I can give them the best of everything and place them in a New York City café.

We both have dreams. We both have sharp minds we're dying to use. We both try to make the best of any situation and open any door possible. We both love and sacrifice anything for our children.

We all cry. We all bleed. We all love. We all laugh. Some of us just have more open doors; more possibilities.

God, you see the disparity between us.

So today, I lift up this prayer for these Kurdish women and their families:

Let them experience your grace, even stronger.
Your love, even deeper.
Your presence, even greater.
And, please give that little boy a voice.

Chapter Eight
Hope for a Kurdish Woman

I have seen many needs in Armenia. All you have to do is turn on the television or open the cover of *TIME* magazine to see the world is hurting. The quality of life in developing countries around the globe is poor, and that, unfortunately, is a dismal reflection on all of us who "have." The eyes that stare back at us in a photographic image do not have a voice. And many of them don't know they don't "have." But ... I do. And the villages of Armenia are full of such people.

I have seen people who have lived 20 years in shipping containers that were used to bring over aid after the 1988 earthquake. Promises were never kept to get them into a real home. I've seen countless homes heated by a stove full of cow dung in the midst of a bitter, cold winter. Disabled children sit in squalid orphanages, abandoned at birth due to their conditions and parents who felt overwhelmed in a nation where they have no support.

These are all difficult things to experience—especially when I compare the memories I have of growing up in prosperous America to the lives many people endure.

I graduated high school in 1996. The Armenians talk about that year and the ones that surround it as the "Dark Years." Communism had fallen. Their infrastructure had broken apart. They were cutting down every tree and stripping every park bench in sight to find wood to heat their homes. They were given two hours or rationed electricity a day. Students often studied by candlelight, and walked home at night, after classes, along unlit streets filled with the unknown.

What was I doing in 1996?

I was applying for college scholarships, busy with schoolwork, attending chilly fall football games and planning my graduation open house. My biggest dilemma was making sure there would be enough tortilla chips to feed all the hungry guests who would arrive at my home with Dr. Suess' *Oh the Places You'll Go* in hand.

Since being in Armenia, I've often thought about the differences between Armenians and me. But, fundamentally, there is only one difference—I was born in America and they were born in Armenia.

The world is, for the most part, open to me and my American passport. My education and job opportunities are somewhat limitless.

Most Armenians cannot get a visa to travel anywhere out of the former Soviet Union. Many have dreamed of higher education, but lacked money for tuition. Others would love to have a decent paying job or a chance to start a business, but they've lost hope in the face of true impossibilities that stand sternly in their paths.

I know that they have passed through valleys that I have never been forced to set foot in, and they have developed a spirit of perseverance I may never possess. This truth always lingered in the back of my mind, but I was never moved to do something about it until I saw her.

I have traveled to the Kurdish villages many times, but in March 2010, I was invited to have coffee with the neighbors of a Kurdish pastor. Our host, Pastor Baris, had introduced nearly every household in his village to Christ—except his neighbor's.

That day I saw "me" in the Kurdish Village. She was a young wife in her 20s. She was cowering in a corner; would not speak; no eye contact. It was obvious she had been beaten down. She had worked hard every day of her three-year marriage to please her husband's parents. She did all their laundry by hand, cleaned their home, made the food, and never said a word. Her in-laws proudly showed me the dowry she had brought into their home on her wedding day.

However, I quickly discovered she had not succeeded in doing what they desired most: produce a child. She was about to be turned out of her husband's home and returned to her father, rejected, with no hope of remarrying. She would bring shame on her family, and there were stories of such daughters being killed to eradicate the perceived curse.

I realized that if I had been born to this Kurdish family in Armenia, her fate would have been mine. I have an infertility disease, and without intervention, I wouldn't have been able to have children. I would have been scorned and thrown out; no hope of a future.

I left the village, and her face was burned in my memory.

As we drove home through the mountainous roads back to Yerevan,

Nick played his usual podcasts to help the ride pass quickly. Today was different. Instead of staring out the window, as my melancholy mind got lost in its own thoughts, I listened to the words of Andy Stanley.

"You can't help everyone equally, but don't let that stop you from helping the one with whom you can truly make a difference."

I felt like God was telling me that I could not just walk away, forget her face; her situation. I had to do everything in my power to help her.

Months passed, and then I had the opportunity to revisit that home with a doctor from America. The doctor was able to discuss her specific situation and give her a plan. We met with her. We met with her husband. We broke tradition and decided not to meet with the interfering mother-in-law. We were able to pray with them and I knew the visit gave them a hope that God has heard this Kurdish woman's cries for a child that would not only be her family's future, but her future.

God's miracles are everywhere. They are not always displayed for all to marvel at. In a small green and white wallpapered room, I witnessed a miracle. The couple grabbed hands and acknowledged their need for God, committed to follow the doctor's plan, and believed that God would give them the gift of a home filled with the sound of barefoot feet and children's laughter.

That was my wish for this woman.

That is the wish God granted for me.

American or Kurd—we are not all that different.

Chapter Nine

216 Smiles

It was a sunny fall day in Yerevan. I woke up early, dressed Ava in her cutest dress, and began the bumpy twenty-minute ride from our home to the city center. It was a Saturday morning and the streets were bare; waiting for the Armenians to awake from their late Friday night bedtimes. But I knew that I was not the only one that was up and preparing for this big day.

Today was the culmination of years of effort—the translation of textbooks, the hosting of American professors, the oversight of three church unions as they had all gathered to finally have a chance to study. In a few hours I would stand on the stage of the Marriott Hotel in Armenia and watch 216 students receive their Bachelor's degrees in Theological Studies.

I had awakened early to do what any Armenian woman would do on a celebratory day like this one—get my hair professionally styled. I sat in the salon, keeping an eye on Ava, her chubby legs tottering around as she charmed every adult in the room. I visualized 216 smiles—every student standing in front of a bedroom mirror, preparing for graduation day.

Each smile was unique—some young, some old. Some were reserved while others were extravagant, practically bursting at the seams. Their smiles even seemed to outshine their newly purchased black suits and dresses. The black graduation gowns were well-ironed. The traditional square caps were strategically placed atop each person's ahead so as to not interfere with the carefully styled hair they had just paid precious money for at the salon.

I remembered the anticipation I felt on my high school graduation day. After enduring 13 years of anticipation and hard work, I said goodbye to friends and classmates whom I met on the kindergarten playground. Within a few months, I would tear away from family, from a familiar hometown, and begin all over again. I walked up on stage, I was handed my diploma, and I felt the burden of all of those years of hard work and study be lifted off of me, and all I could do was smile.

University brought new challenges and greater self-reliance. Five years of intense study passed, and I had finally written the 60- page English literature thesis paper and performed a nerve-racking senior vocal and piano recital. The morning of graduation I woke up and looked out the brick-encased windows of my on-campus apartment to see the streets I had walked to and from class so many times. I could not believe my graduation day had finally arrived.

A few hours later, I stood in my black graduation gown and cap, with a golden tassel hanging, as I sang in my university choir one last time to open the ceremony. I walked up on stage to receive my diploma and smiled for a photo as I shook our president's hand. All my professors in their doctoral garb surrounded me and once again, I felt a burden lift. I was finished, and all I could do was smile.

In September 2010, I was the official standing on stage to shake each graduate's hand. What a privilege to award diplomas to 216 Armenian students.

Some were young and eager to begin their future. Others were pastors in their 50s and 60s, ministers who had shared the love of Christ when it was forbidden under Communism. They were the pastors who had laid a foundation of the church and they finally had a chance to get the education they desired and deserved.

I watched as each student's name was called, and the tassel swayed back and forth in rhythm with each excited step. Many tried to hold back their smile; to remain in control of their face; to stay serious and dignified for the event. It may have been easier under different circumstances with less historical significance. But they all failed.

Some of the most seasoned pastors, those denied their religious freedom by Soviet occupiers, had tears in their eyes as they finally grasped their diploma, a long awaited victory.

As I stood on the stage, I determined to look deeply into the eyes of each student, one-by-one. They had accomplished something that seemed impossible, and I was granted the best vantage point to witness their commencement.

216 Armenians that finished the course.

216 framed, cherished diplomas.

216 unwritten futures.

All we could do was smile—a glorious, proud and carefree smile.

Chapter Ten

Remember Marina

Nine years ago, we stepped off the airplane into our new life in Armenia. The unfamiliar summer air blew in our faces, and our eyes squinted to find our welcome committee of a few Americans amidst the sea of cigarette smoke.

The Congress Hotel in Yerevan became our temporary home, and it was piled high with our suitcases and Rubbermaid tubs filled with all we had for our new life. In a few days, our American friends returned home and we felt lost and homeless. The clutter spilling out of our suitcases matched the chaos inside as we looked for a house, language lessons and a familiar bite to eat. We were alone.

On our first Sunday, we attended a church service. We sat in a crowded sanctuary resigned to the fact that we couldn't read a single word or understand anything that was spoken. By the puzzled look on our faces, and Nick's six-foot plus stature towering above a sea of Armenians, it was obvious to everyone that we were not native. What could have been just another day of cultural immersion turned out to be a morning I would never forget, the morning I met Marina.

She walked up to us in an all-white pantsuit and boots with five-inch heels. Her long jet-black hair was in sharp contrast to her outfit, but it was the playfulness of her pink sunglasses hiding her incredibly long eyelashes that intrigued me. I immediately turned to Nick and said, under my breath, "I think she's one of the most beautiful girls I've ever seen."

She translated for us that day when we were invited up on the church's stage to greet the congregation. We could have never imagined the great role she would have in our future.

A few years later, on my birthday, Marina gave me a beautiful necklace. Its pendant revealed a silver, hand-carved pomegranate, one of the national symbols of Armenia, encased in a circle of deep red. I had admired this necklace before and knew that the cost of this thoughtful gift was more money than she had. As she handed it to me she said, "You are my best friend."

I hadn't thought of having a best friend since high school, but as Marina looked at me with her sincere eyes, I realized that she was my closest friend too. She became the foundation of everything we did. I cannot imagine our years in Armenia without her tireless work, listening ear and life-giving wisdom.

One of Marina's most important achievements was the work she did at the Bible college. She was so meticulous and sharp that any executive in America would be fortunate to have Marina by his or her side, bringing it all together. Her organizational skills made the logistical nightmare of overseeing the Bible college and the huge translation task possible. The irony was the she did not have the opportunity to study in the program.

September 24, 2010

All the smiling faces had walked across the stage and received their diplomas; feeling an incomparable pride in their achievement. I looked over at Marina from the stage. Standing over in the corner, she looked exhausted. She had just organized an entire graduation, dinner reception and corralled 216 students into an organized line.

Her voice was gone. Her feet hurt. Her tireless energy had synchronized a memorable day for everyone but her. She smiled back at me the loveliest of smiles that hid her aching heart.

Suddenly, I called her up on stage. I said a word of thanks—probably something Marina expected. Then, I pulled out a blue leather cover with the words "North Central University" embellished in gold. She had no idea what was about to happen, and she had no context to understand what I held in my hands.

I couldn't feign a tone of seriousness. I was now tearing up as a smile spread itself across my face. "Marina Stepanyan has been awarded an Honorary Bachelor's Degree in Organizational Leadership from my Alma Mater, North Central University."

She stood there for just a second as her mind unraveled what exactly was happening. Her hands covered her face; she looked up in complete disbelief.

Hopefully all of us have had those moments when we experience some act of unexpected grace, and we feel as if someone is smiling down on us from heaven. He knows us. He knows what we do; what we sacrifice. He remembers.

God did a miracle on Marina's behalf and reminded her that He truly does see everything. He had worked to convince an American university's cabinet to approve this degree for, in my opinion, the most deserving woman I've ever met.

So, on that day, we celebrated 216 graduates and we celebrated Marina! We celebrated her tireless investment in our family and in the kingdom of God in Armenia. We celebrated God's ever-searching eye that notices the hidden things and evaluates our motives and ambitions. And, most of all, we celebrated His extravagant grace.

"Just as lotions and fragrances bring delight,
a sweet friendship refreshes the soul."
—Proverbs 27:9, The Message

Chapter Eleven

The Act of Serving

June 16, 2003

The warmth of summer was settling on the city, and the famous Chicago wind blew strongly as we pulled our luggage out of my parents' van and into O'Hare airport. Hugging my family one last time and quickly checking to make sure we had our passports and tickets, we boarded the plane that would take us on the first leg of our journey.

Chicago to Washington D.C.

Washington D.C. to Vienna

Vienna to Yerevan

36 long hours

I didn't know when I would return.

The captain announced our descent in to Yerevan, gave the weather report, and thanked us for flying with Austrian Airlines. I looked through the small window to catch a view of Yerevan. It was pitch black below. I scanned the horizon. Nothing. I look down. One tiny white light beamed a humble greeting. Panic. Where was Yerevan, the capital city? A capital city of a nation has only one light? Where was I moving?

September 10, 2010 – Artavaz Village

I am standing in one of those villages that I'm sure I passed over on my initial descent into Armenia. The main road is completely broken apart, and the waste of sheep and cows is littered everywhere. One light stands on a pole that leans to the left so as not to over-illuminate the conditions below. Surprisingly, I look up into the sky, and I THANK GOD that I am here. Sitting with the women and children, I breathe in the scent of the village air; so different from the breeze in Chicago on the day I left for America. My clothes and hair absorb the strong perfume on the ladies, and we all become one.

I continue to whisper quiet thank yous to God. Thank you that I was able to learn this language. Thank you that I can sit and talk with every single person I come in contact with. Thank you that I can DO something. Thankful that I am here.

Thank you for this wonderful team of 12 Armenian women who have left the major cities and who are with me, joyfully serving this village. They gave of their limited money to pay for all of their expenses, and left helpless husbands and crying children behind. Our goal was to serve, love, listen and expose them to the simple love of God.

To show that God cares for even the mundane chores of life, we went into their fields and dug potatoes from the ground. As we worked, we were entertained by our constant companions—hungry children anticipating bowls of steaming food on their dinner table. Our tender hands brought in the fall harvest for three families.

Hearing of a desperately sick woman from the villagers, we went to her home and cleaned it from floor to ceiling. Her best crystal was finally able to shine again, and she could live in a place that she was no longer ashamed of; a portion of her dignity restored.

We sang, played games with the young at heart, and shared stories from the Bible to children sitting cross-legged on a dirt floor, thankful for a diversion from chores. We enjoyed cake, tea and coffee with the women, sharing stories about families and God's love. I smiled as I realized that this experience was no different than sitting across my kitchen table with my friends in Minneapolis—sweets, laughter and the need to be heard above the noise of the world.

Serving others changes us. It aligns us with Jesus and what He is doing in the world. Through our hands, He feeds the hungry—both physically and spiritually. My prayer is that we did something during our three days to illuminate a dark place. We planted a seed in the soil we harvested, allowing God's kingdom to take root.

Our hope, as we served in Armenia, was to make a difference. As I look back on my years there, I realize that the biggest changes occurred in me. Thank God that as we serve others, He works on us. When we look out on a dark land filled with such little light, we can trust that He will use us as one flickering candle in a place He loves so much.

I will never be the same.

Chapter Twelve

Returning Home: The Story of Hranush

Publishers learned long ago the persuasive power of a well-designed book cover. From the artwork to the texture of the material used to bind, the visual appeal of a book in hand can lead us to open the pages or put it back on the shelf. How many of us remember a grandma reciting the old adage, "You can't judge a book by its cover."

In her ageless wisdom she was telling us that the beautiful and popular do not always make for a steadfast friend, and to not overlook the unassuming where a treasure could reside. My friend, Hranush, is one of those rare people.

I met Hranush five years ago when she applied to be a part of our team of translators and editors who worked to translate a study Bible. She is more widely known as a newscaster on the capital city's news station.

Hranush is sharp. Fashionable. Strong. Quiet. If she were to walk into any room in Armenia, everyone would assume that she is from an influential Armenian family that gave her all the possibilities in the world to rise to success. At first glance, the cover of Hranush's life story would allude to privilege. But don't judge a book by its cover.

In 2010, we were driving the long, three-hour journey to the village of Jujevan when she first told me her story. I was leading another group of eight women to serve in the village by cleaning, gardening and by doing anything else we could do. This was not a group of American volunteers, but a group of Armenian women who paid their way to go and serve the most needy in their nation, to show the tangible love of Christ.

But this was Hranush's village. This was the village she once fled from, leaving a difficult life behind. Now an irresistible force was pulling her back to serve and to bless, and we had the privilege of accompanying her.

While passing burned-out border villages, destroyed during the recent war with Azerbaijan, I, being the dramatic person that I am, asked a question to everyone in my car, "Have any of you ever been in a bad auto accident?"

The others said no. Hranush said, "Yes."

This is the point where *most* of us would recount the story, reliving every detail, every emotion. Not Hranush. Just a simple, quiet "yes." After much coaxing, I pulled the story from a hidden place in her heart that I would discover was wrought with pain.

Hranush was a little girl, five years old. Late one evening, she and her family were on their way to a celebration in a nearby village along with 30 or 40 people, shoulder to shoulder in the back of a large open truck.

As the truck wound along the narrow road, past steep rock walls and unguarded drop-offs, the driver fell asleep. The truck rolled over. Most everyone escaped unhurt, but two people remained trapped and crushed under the weight of the truck: Hranush and her sixteen year old sister. Her sister died instantly, but Hranush remained under the truck for more than an hour as they waited for the nearest hospital to send an ambulance.

All she remembered from that night was a group of men trying repeatedly to lift the heavy truck up to pull her out. Each time, their strength was not enough. They would lift it up, and failing to free her, the truck would fall back down on her leg and leave her in crushing, excruciating pain. Finally, Hranush was rescued. She endured many surgeries to rebuild her leg, and her path to recovery was tedious.

Hranush was one of five children before she lost her older sister that day. Although her mother was not a young woman, she determined to replace the deep loss of her teenage daughter by conceiving once again. When the day finally came to deliver, Hranush's mother died giving birth to a son. In a moment of time, one life ended and another took his first breath.

Hranush's father, clothed in grief, left his new son behind and reluctantly returned home to tell his children that their mother and new brother had died. He now stood in a motherless house full of children. He could not look into their trusting, brown eyes and tell them the truth—that he could not endure raising yet another child without the companionship of his loving wife. To this day, no one truly knows what became of Hranush's baby brother.

Eager for help, her father soon remarried, and this new stepmother made the rest of Hranush's years at home a living nightmare she couldn't wait to escape.

God intervened—a reminder of the way He cares for us in ways unimaginable from our limited perspective. He saw a miserable girl, educated in a rural village. Although the chains of poverty were shackled around her, God opened the door for her to attend one of the top universities in Armenia.

This was miraculous news. Everyone was overjoyed—everyone except her father. He forbade her to go, and her culture dictated that by willfully leaving she would bring shame to his already weakened pride. He threatened to disown her and without money and the support of her father, all hope disappeared.

Thankfully, impossible is not a word in God's vocabulary. Amidst hundreds of students, Hranush was one of a handful that was granted a full scholarship. With God's will for her life clearly set before her, Hranush took the final step. She walked through the door of her father's home, and treaded one last time down the familiar village dirt paths lined by make-shift fences and time-worn trees to board a bus for the city. With every kilometer the bus traveled, she left behind a difficult family situation and the village way of life. Hranush set her heart on her future and never looked back.

Today, Hranush is a successful professional. Something deep within her, a determination as strong as steel, turned a small ray of hope into a career, and opened doors that are beyond the hopes of thousands who never leave the confines of small village life.

Hranush knows she has reached this place because God recognized her struggle and was her constant companion—in the village lanes and in the city streets.

October 16, 2010 – Jujevan Village

We sat in the office of the mayor of Jujevan. It is quickly obvious that Hranush is a local celebrity. Everyone stands when she enters the room and a special seat awaits her at the head of the mayor's conference table. Hranush humbly smiles at the compliments, but then politely guides the discussion to the most needy families in the village. How can we help?

A woman by the name of Sylva comes up in our conversation. Then the mayor searches Hranush's face, and asks, "Is it ok if we work with her?"

Hranush replies without hesitancy, "Sure. Of course."

A few minutes later, Sylva walks into the room. She is one of a group of village women gathered by the mayor to speak with us and share coffee and conversation. Village life demanded unending chores, and it was time to bring in the fall harvest. They seemed grateful for such a great excuse to leave home and gather with Hranush, a few Americans, and a piece of sweet cake brought from one of the best bakeries in the capital city, Yerevan. I was given the privilege of speaking to them.

I shared about my life in Armenia and the great things that Armenians have taught me over the years. I told stories of how Armenians have reached out to us—a foreign family who attempted to live, speak Armenian and serve in their country. Then I shared with them about the love that God has for them. I remind them that they are not in a forgotten place, and that He is walking with them. Hranush shared a bit of her story, how she discovered full life in Christ, and the evidence that God is her constant companion.

I look around the room at their worn faces. I can see a flicker of hope in many of their eyes. One of the leaders in the village—a strong, outspoken woman—shares her story and begged answers to ominous questions. She cried as she sought to understand the injustice she had experienced in the village. But as we confidently reassured her of God's love and purpose, our whole team sensed that something changed in her, as if a heavy weight had lifted.

Then Sylva spoke up. She had tears in her eyes. With a tired voice she thanked us for coming and for showing her that she is not alone.

The final thing I did that weekend was walk the muddy village roads with Sylva. Her husband, I learned, was the truck driver from that life-changing night established deep in the memory of the village. It meant so much to Sylva, to everyone, that *Hranush* had returned.

> *"God blesses those who are poor and realize their need for him, for the Kingdom of Heaven is theirs.*
> *God blesses those who mourn, for they will be comforted.*
> *God blesses those who are humble, for they will inherit the whole earth.*
> *God blesses those who hunger and thirst for justice, for they will be satisfied.*
> *God blesses those who are merciful, for they will be shown mercy.*
> *God blesses those whose hearts are pure, for they will see God."*
> *—Matthew 5: 4, 7–9, New Living Translation*

A Baby for Delor

When many hear the words "developing country," most people are not alarmed. They visualize an impoverished nation that is being revitalized through the construction of new homes and stores, better medical care and schools. They imagine the population will one day soon experience the same comforts and standard of living the West enjoys. But in reality, those words are actually a polite way to say something far different. And in the developing nation of Armenia, poverty can be found everywhere. When you see it so often, it is easy to become desensitized to the well-worn shoes, torn and dirty clothing and the begging, desperate eyes that plead with you every day.

A clandestine meeting with Delor, the Kurdish woman found cowering in the shadows of her husband's home, awoke me from my apathy. Childless, she was facing rejection from her entire family and was about to be returned to her father's home in shame. I knew I had to help her.

As we sat around a small table adorned with Armenian coffee and old, melted chocolates, Delor's mother-in-law told us that she was tired of hearing Delor cry herself to sleep every night while praying for a child. She kept the floors spotless, the house warm, the dinners ready. She strived for perfection, anything to earn a permanent place in the home. But, none of that was enough. A child must be born!

Delor's in-laws had taken her to a doctor who confirmed the problem was hers alone. This diagnosis was brought into doubt when, during our medical seminars with the Kurds that week, a group of women, my age, confided that all of their husbands could be found in the arms of prostitutes from the neighboring village weekly. Following the bad example set by the other men of the village, Delor's husband only desired to be intimate with her about once a month, on the day that he chose. Yet, she was the one to blame.

The American doctor met with the young couple. They committed to strategically try to have a child and both acknowledged a need for God in their lives. We prayed for healing and that God would allow them to hear the sound of little feet echo in their home.

As we left that day, Delor looked me in the eye, whispered her thanks to me and took my hand in hers before returning to her dark corner next to the furnace. My heart broke thinking of her, left here with what seemed to be such a weak flicker of hope. I couldn't bare the thought of letting it die.

Without thinking through the implications, I made a promise. If Delor and her husband followed the doctor's plan and still did not have a child in six months, then I would take her to my fertility doctor in Armenia's capital city.

Six busy months passed and I found myself afraid to return to the little run-down house in the Kurdish village. I was afraid to find that Delor had lost hope. I feared that if I took her to treatment, and it was confirmed that she had an untreatable physical problem, that she would immediately be cast out of her home. Or, perhaps, I would return to find that she had already been rejected and alone in her father's house. But, I knew I had to do something—her eyes, her shadow, her story.

In April 2011, as we drove the road to her village, I was praying for guidance. Praying for wisdom. Lacking faith. When I walked into the door of her home, a flash of recognition lit up Delor's face and she smiled at me. She grabbed my hand firmly between her two hands and whispered hello.

Her toothless and desperately thin mother-in-law proudly proclaimed, "Delor is four months pregnant! We were going to cast her out of our home this very month if she did not produce a child. But she's a good wife. She's expecting!"

Oh, God. Why did I come expecting the barren?

But here in this remote village, in a nation that most have never heard of, you heard the cries of a young woman. You felt the tear-stained pillow as she whispered prayers to you in the night. You, amidst the billions of people in the world, looked down and saw Delor.

Soon those old, cracked wooden floors of that Kurdish home will be filled with the sounds of jumping, running, and the walls will resonate with laughter!

You are a God that removes our barrenness. You mold us. You strengthen us. You carry us through the difficulty. And then You whisper to us that You were the quiet presence walking with us all along the treacherous road.

When it was time to leave Delor's home that day, she followed me outside, put her hand on my arm and whispered a quiet thanks. A whisper was the only way that her culture allowed her to speak to those with higher social status. Even in the whisper, the joy bubbling up inside of her was unmistakable. Soon, she will be irreplaceable in that family. Delor will be the mother of the only grandchild and the only future that meager family has.

In Delor's story we can all find hope. God does not regard the comfortable mansions of the rich, or hold counsel with a self-appointed intellectual.

He is found in the poorest streets,
in the hearts of the searching,
in the words of the humble,
in the deeds of the truly kind,
in the unquestionable faith of a child, and
in the tear-filled nights of a forgotten Kurdish woman.

> *"The LORD always keeps his promises; he is gracious in all he does.*
> *The LORD helps the fallen and lifts those bent beneath their loads.*
> *The eyes of all look to you in hope; you give them their food as they need it.*
> *When you open your hand, you satisfy the hunger and thirst of*
> *every living thing.*
> *The LORD is righteous in everything he does; he is filled with kindness.*
> *The LORD is close to all who call on him, yes, to all who call on him in truth.*
> *He grants the desires of those who fear him; he hears their cries for*
> *help and rescues them."*
> *—Psalm 145:13-19, New Living Translation*

Part Three
Culture

Chapter Fourteen

Culture Shock

It is such a comfort to wake up in America as an American. You know the language and you can interpret people's glances, smiles or under-the-breath huffs. You know how to wait in line and negotiate. You can identify a dime out of a fist full of quarters, pennies and nickels without a second's delay. You can drive and daydream at the same time, responding to the rules of the road with confidence.

It is like returning to your parents' home and sleeping in your old bedroom. The stuffed animals and games have been put away, but as you lay in your bed and stare at the familiar crack in the ceiling plaster you know a quick jaunt to the attic can retrieve everything you loved years ago.

Living outside of your culture is like going through your day with a constant, unseen resistance, as if you were wading through water with each step. For eight years in Armenia, I would complete each day with a feeling of complete exhaustion. Especially during the first few years, Nick and I would collapse and wonder what had sapped our youthful energy.

As an American attempting to describe the culture of Armenia, some of the first contrasts that come to mind are the negative ones. Our many guests would immediately point out many of them after a few short hours in the country.

"They don't know how to wait in lines! They practically run me over when I'm crossing the street. Can you believe she just told me I had gained weight? Why are they staring at me? Who taught these people to drive, anyway? Come on, deodorant doesn't cost that much!"

And unfortunately, in times of stress and exhaustion, the list could go on and on and on. Then comes a good night's sleep, a reset of a weary heart, and a prayer to God, "Fill me with your love and give me perspective."

Overcoming culture shock is like raising a challenging son. We try to mold the child's will and lecture him on how he should act. We send him stern glances across the room and hope he understands the need to change his behavior. But, ultimately, we finally realize that we can only truly influence him once we love and accept him for who he is.

Every person, every culture, has its own beauty. We can choose to be blinded by the challenges, or we can choose to find the gift that each beholds, instilled by God, and let it thrive. This chapter is dedicated to the wonderful culture I discovered after I finally looked past the superficial and discovered the beauty of the Armenian people.

The Importance of Children

Armenians are survivors. They have fought for centuries to preserve their land, their language and their church from invading empires. From this perseverant culture came a deep love of the nation's true treasure and key to survival—their children. Raising children in Armenia revealed a part of their culture that endeared this land to our heart. Children were never seen as a disruption or an annoying clamor. Every member of a family, uncles and aunts, cousins and even neighbors, cherished a child in the home as if it was their own. The love of children is such a deeply rooted value that kidnapping and abuse is seldom heard of.

This cultural difference was tangibly felt when I walked on to a plane full of Armenians with one of my babies. As they saw our chubby little Ava being carried down the aisle, inevitably we would hear them chatter.

"How wonderful! How delicious! Look, blue eyes! Oh my goodness!"

They would lean in to kiss her hands and make a silly face to capture Ava's laughter. It was just a matter of time before candy would come from all directions. In contrast, when Americans notice a baby as they board an airplane, paranoia ensues.

In Armenia, children are never an inconvenience, and families would plead with me to have the opportunity to babysit my children—if only for a few hours. They would turn their homes and kitchens upside down to find the perfect food or toys to please their little Puccini guests.

Nick and I could have a date night at a nice restaurant with our young children and be confident that their presence would brighten the atmosphere. The Armenian waiter would ask permission to proudly carry our light-haired, blue-eyed children around on their hip and give them a tour of the kitchen. Thirty minutes later, after hearing many oohs and ahhs, they would return our child, small gift in hand, from the kitchen.

Oliver was nine months old the first time we had planned to return home to America for Christmas. Due to the extreme fog in Yerevan, we were called the evening before our flight and told that the plane had been forced to land at the airport in Tbilisi, Georigia, a four-hour drive through the mountains north of us. It was already nine in the evening when we began to franticly pack our suitcases for a month back home. After hiring a taxi at midnight, we began the three-hour drive to the border. Through our exhaustion, we attempted to juggle the difficult task of pushing a stroller and our luggage across an icy bridge that served as a border crossing.

Once we arrived on the Georgian side of the border, we were met with a line of tour buses filled with passengers also desperately trying to make their early morning flights. We approached a small rusty trailer, and Nick took our passports inside to be processed. Inside sat a Georgian border officer behind a small metal desk, bundled tightly in a wool coat, a large Russian fur hat crowned his head. There was a television blaring in the corner, and a small wood-burning stove heated the room. Stacked on top of his desk were piles of passports. He entered the passport numbers, one by one, and waited as the dial-up modem sent and retrieved information. Each passport took an eternity.

After a few minutes, Nick leaned out of the trailer and said, "I have an idea! Bring Oliver inside." We entered the trailer and the officer looked up to see us.

In that instant, this giant of a man melted before our eyes. Without hesitation, he stood to his feet, walked out from behind his desk, and came face to face with our little baby boy.

"Ki-ki-ki-ki-ki … ki-ki-ki-ki-ki …. ki-ki-ki-ki-ki!"

A huge gold-toothed grin appeared on his face. He sat back down, pushed everything aside and began processing our passports. Within minutes, our pages were stamped and we were on our way to the airport.

When an Armenian loves a child, they will grab the baby's cheeks and say, "I'm gonna eat you up!" For them, children truly are on the delicious side of life. Raising our children in their youngest years in Armenia was such a blessing. They felt completely loved and cherished, and managed to acquire quite a collection of candy, toys and hugs along the way.

Hyurasirutyun - Loving the Guest

Armenian humor says that after the great flood, their ancestors greeted a hungry Noah with a table full of food and wine when he stepped of the ark in the mountains of Ararat. Although obviously a humorous myth, it reveals the Armenians' commitment to give the guest a place of honor—no matter the difficult circumstances!

When I first arrived in Yerevan, I missed the generous smiles and greetings that Americans often will give to friends and strangers alike. As I walked through the streets of Armenia, I would attempt to make eye contact and greet passers-by with a genuine smile. They returned my gaze, wondering whether they should know me or not, their mouths would remain rigid, and they walked on by.

At first I comforted myself with the thought that perhaps women didn't return my kind gesture due to the pain they were forced to endure as they walked uneven streets in five-inch heels. But, my doubts were confirmed when I attempted to pay our telephone bill at the local post office. I approached the glass window, used my limited Armenian and attempted to win the tired postal worker over with a good American smile.

No smile in return. Just a look that broke any language barrier and communicated with me very clearly, "I have work to do. Pay your bill and move out of line!"

Then I had the chance to enter an Armenian's home for dinner. Suddenly I realized that the Soviet Empire had taught this flamboyant people group to remain stoic in public. Communism could not, however, kill the generosity and joy that resides in the Armenians' hearts once they are inside the secure walls of their homes.

The hosts invited us into a meticulously cleaned home, and sat us at a table that was set with great care and adorned with the family's best lace tablecloth and china. Napkins were carefully folded into perfect triangular designs amidst glass pitchers filled with homemade apricot and cherry juice compotes.

The clock would suddenly stop ticking as the tables were filled with eggplant walnut rolls, various cheeses and greens from the garden. The bright colors stood in contrast to the white pile of bread that was stacked by each guest's plate. Once the main entrée arrived, the hostess attempted to stack and balance the various platters filled with meat, salads and side dishes. A full and crowded table bought out her delightful smile. She enjoyed the extravagance of the event—a whole week's normal food budget was spent to generously feed her guests.

The meal is somewhat of an epic battle. The hostess fills the cups and plates, and if her sharp eye notices the enjoyment of one of her dishes, she proudly fills the guests' plates with that favored commodity again and again. This evening was not a waste of time, and the extravagant meal was not an unwise use of their modest income. It was a roll-out-the-red-carpet special occasion.

The wealth of this hospitality has inspired me to always make my guests, expected or unexpected, feel loved and appreciated. My habits have changed. I find myself freezing loaves of banana bread and cookie dough so baked goods can be ready in a matter of minutes when an unexpected guest stops by. The Armenians taught me to sit back, relax and be extravagant with my time, resources and hospitality. They truly are the experts!

The Value of People

Hospitality is an expertise the Armenians have polished over centuries, but perhaps their open-handed generosity actually arose from times of despair. Through their decades of hardship, they have learned the true value of life—people.

My wonderful language teacher, Jasmina, once told me a bit of her nation's story. The first year after the collapse of the Soviet Union, Armenia's nuclear power plant and main industries could no longer function without the interdependent system the Soviet Union had developed. The country endured a year without electricity. The families and neighbors came together to pass the evenings in the shadow of candlelight. The dark rooms of their homes would echo with laughter and the joy of one another's company.

Even though those difficult years have passed and electricity has become predictable, the core of this Armenian value remains the same. Modern-day conveniences could be stripped away from them once again, and they would still survive on the wealth they possess in their families, their friends and their nation. When everything else fades, relationship is most important.

This value is engrained in them, and the Armenian culture outwardly shows its love with friends. Greetings are sealed with a kiss and best friends walk down the prominent streets hand-in-hand. They show their love in a simple grasp of your hand as you cross a busy street, in the latch of your arm during a dinner, and an invitation to dance with them under the beat of loud music and the scat of a traditional Middle Eastern singer.

At first, I was uncomfortable with an Armenian woman holding my hand as we strolled through the streets of Yerevan. Not the most affectionate person, I felt rigid. Nick's advice?

"When they grab your hand, throw all caution to the wind, and grab back even harder."

This lesson rings true for every person who experiences the gift of living abroad. Our natural inclination is to climb into a secure lifeboat when the flow of culture that surrounds us becomes too threatening. Rather, jump into the stream, feel the exhaustion of the swim become easier with each passing day. And when an Armenian reaches out their hand to invite you along the current, you grab back harder.

Chapter Fifteen

Reverse Culture Shock? Really?

When Nick and I were preparing to move overseas, we sat in classes, read books and talked with veteran missionaries about culture shock. We knew it wasn't like sticking your finger in an electrical socket, but we were beginning to get the idea that moving from one country to another was a shock to the system nonetheless. We flew into culture shock head-on when we landed in Armenia, but what was even more curious to us was the concept of "reverse culture shock." No books or lectures on that one—just a plain, smack you in the face jolt into a previous reality.

Many of my expat friends have described their reverse culture shock experiences. After years of shopping in outdoor markets or small, one-room stores, they arrive back home to the United States and immediately make their way to the nearest Super Target. They are overwhelmed with the variety: 100s of different cereal options, an aisle full of different breads, 30 types of mustard and 20 brands of barbeque sauce (a rarity in most countries). Overwhelmed by the sheer extravagance of it all, their eyes fill up with tears and they leave the store.

When I first heard this, I thought, "What in the world are they talking about?" We have grown up in America and a few years can't erase what we have experienced our entire lives. Home should be the most comforting and familiar place in the world to us. WE ARE AMERICANS, AFTER ALL.

I must admit that every time I return home it isn't long before I make a trip to Target, circling the aisles with my shiny red cart. As I toss shampoo into my cart, I wait for a panic attack. I have a tissue in my pocket to dab my tears but nothing happens. I don't feel overwhelmed. Skipping gleefully down the aisle, I grab a tube of toothpaste twice as large as the one I can buy in Armenia, and thank God I am home.

Through my nine years of living abroad, I have visited America several times. I am like a guest now, with no home to call my own. I rely on the generosity of family and friends to provide a pillow and a bed for my jet-lagged body. Outside the ground is covered with the freezing snow of a Minnesota winter, but I am bundled up in my down-filled coat and cozy shearling boots. I awake, turn on "Good Morning, America" and feel like an American once again.

On a whim, Nick used our precious airline reward points and let me fly back for five days in Chicago. I showed up on the doorstep of my sister's old brick apartment building, completely surprising her for her 30th birthday. On this visit I kept a blog diary and after rereading it at home in Armenia, I realized Chicago had offered me some reverse culture shock. As I walked the streets and observed everyday life, I felt the clash of the East and West for the first time.

Where is the invisible line that splits me in two and makes me feel like a "nowhere man?" I don't know, but as I cling to my "American me" I am not sure how tightly I want to hold on. Here are some stories I wrote on my blog during the trip.

Reverse Culture Shock # 1: Lines

Americans LOVE lines.

We love the orderliness of them. We love the fairness and justice we feel while waiting in one. We are taught the importance of them from a very young age. During our early years, how many of our daily educational minutes are spent on teaching our American children how to quietly and patiently line up and wait in a line?

A line to walk to music class. A line to get a drink at the water fountain. Line up to take a turn to climb the rope in gym class. Lines at Disney World. Lines at McDonald's. Lines at the grocery store check-out counters. Lines at government offices. Lines while driving.

Lines. Lines. Lines.

Well, lines work well in North America, Europe and probably Australia. But once you leave the Western world, forget about it!

When I first arrived in Armenia, my inherently American desire for the world to operate in a system of lines would drive me insane. I would be waiting in line at a store to check-out, and an elderly woman would just walk right in front of me to pay for her bag of goods. I felt inwardly enraged but everyone else behind me was calm. She was elderly and had paid her dues. She deserves respect, and she DOES NOT have to wait in lines.

They don't drive "in the lines" in Armenia. Every day I drive, I encounter countless cars that are driving with the dotted line right beneath the center of their car. They are not in one lane or the other...just in the middle of both!

Despite my American-ness, over the last several years, I have learned to relax a bit about lines. There was no decision to make. Either I learned to relax or I would live my life in complete frustration.

October 21, 2010

I arrive at Chicago O'Hare airport and walk into the passport control area. I see that there are people entering the hall from two directions. There are a lot of people coming from the left, and I am coming from the right. So, I merge into the "U.S. Citizen" Passport control line.

Suddenly, I am yelled at.

"The line starts back there." A man points back to the left.

I, completely unaware that the line had grown outside of the large zig-zagging maze and down a hallway, apologize with embarrassment.

"Oh, I'm sorry. I was coming from that direction and thought these two lines merged at the entry way."

Another rude voice from a young lady with glasses, wearing sweat pants; her greasy hair revealing that she had been travelling for a long time.

"Yeah, well, I've been waiting here *forever*," she said as she rolled her tired eyes.

Wow...culture shock! Don't touch the sacredness of the line, even if by mistake. There is no grace! Lines keep the world in order. Lines are egalitarian. In a line, no one is more important or less important than anyone else. My anticipation of a warm welcome by the kindhearted, generous American spirit lay shattered before my passport was ever stamped.

I was both angry and a little sad. What happened to the America that I brag about wherever I go? Where is my grandfather's generation who stands when a lady enters the room, opens a car door, and helps people stranded on the side of the road?

"The line ends back there, lady! Arrrr, Arrrr."

Lines are great. They really do bring fairness and order. But, lines are not more important than people.

Some people do deserve a break: the elderly, the pregnant, the families with young, screaming children who have just endured a transatlantic flight. But in our culture, we don't care. Our sense of fairness and democracy clouds our perspective.

The rest of the world can learn a lot from our systems and organization. There is no doubt that extraordinary inefficiencies are rampant throughout the developing world. And not every American is a soulless automaton. But as a whole, I say we can learn a lot from the rest of the world about compassion, flexibility, and the ability to color outside the lines every now and then.

Reverse Culture Shock # 2: Eating On-the-Go

Americans love to eat "on the go." With the rise of fast food restaurants and drive-thrus, we are a culture that eats while we walk, drive and work at our desk.

Once I was on a marshrutka (public transport van) in Kiev, Ukraine. After standing in the aisle for 20 minutes of the journey, I finally was able to obtain one of the highly coveted seats. I sat down, pulled a granola bar out of my purse and began to eat.

Everyone stared at me. I kept eating.

Everyone continued to stare at me.

Nick leaned over and whispered in my ear, "People don't eat in front of other people like that over here. It's rude. You didn't know that?"

I'm a stubborn person. I looked back up at him and took another deliberate bite out of my granola bar.

I whispered back to him, "I don't care."

Of course, I was not being a good example of someone who is a guest in this country and who was trying to be culturally sensitive. But I was being true to my American self.

A lot of cultures don't have an "eat on the go" mentality, and it is truly difficult for them to understand why we don't have enough time to sit down at a table and eat a normal meal. Why in the world would we eat while riding on a *marshrutka*?

The day before leaving for this trip, I was running errands all over Yerevan and was *starving*. I finally bought a salad, and as I walked around the city center eating it, people stared at me. I continued to eat. I thought... Tomorrow, I'm leaving for America. I can let myself feel American one day early! Then, a man knocked my tabouleh salad out of my hand on to the floor of the post office. It was gone. And with it, the stares disappeared too.

October 22, 2010: My first full day back in America

A prominent display in the produce aisle of Target was pyramided with the largest, reddest apples that I'd seen in a long time. So I bought an apple, walked out the door and began my four-block walk to the subway station. The whole way, I was biting into my juicy apple. Cars drove by, and no one noticed. People passed me on the sidewalk, and didn't stare. I was back in America! For at least a few days, that stubborn little girl inside me was able to eat whenever and wherever she wanted.

Reverse Culture Shock # 3: You Don't Have to Go Far...

Tuesday, October 26, 2010

Every time I return to America, I feel like an awkward teenager trying to desperately relearn the rules of how to dress, act and engage. Mingling with my sister's friends at her 30th birthday party, perhaps there were guests who could sense my uneasiness. Several people approached me and asked me the obligatory, getting-to-know-you question in America: "So what do you do?" Many act surprised by my occupation and immediately began to feel uncomfortable.

"Wow. You work in ARMENIA! Thanks for going over there and helping out!"

Yes, in terms of economic opportunity, it certainly is not as blessed as America. Some people live in abandoned shipping containers left after the 1988 earthquake. Others live in villages with no running water. The average income, nation-wide, is around $300 a month. The need is overwhelming. But this week while riding the subway in Chicago, I was reminded that great need can be found everywhere.

I observed a 50-year-old African American man step on to the train. He had a beard, earrings, wore a hat supporting Barack Obama, jeans and coat made from neon patches. His outfit looked like cartoon characters haphazardly quilted together. Obscenities were airbrushed over his coat of many colors.

His wife entered a few seconds after him. She was a short, Caucasian woman, overweight, with long straggly hair streaked with grey. Her outfit was nearly identical, except for hot pink socks stuffed into silver ballet flats.

He stood on the train, and she sat down, obviously keeping her distance. He suddenly bolted off, as if to get away just as the doors closed. She scrambled to follow.

He disappeared into the underground hallways, as she fought to keep up. I watched as she looked back at me, somewhat ashamed. As she looked at me, I saw fear in her eyes. What if she lost her husband in this underground maze?

I saw them resurface at the next platform. He stood near the tracks, every time she got close to him, he would move away.

The scene was so bizarre, but for some reason I saw past their caricatures to the humanity that lie beneath. How does it feel to be someone's ball and chain? How does it feel to do everything to be loved by someone, to be accepted, and yet still feel unloved?

My heart reached out to her. Her countenance told her story. She wanted to be loved and accepted and was even running after it.

Yes, most in Armenia don't enjoy the prosperity and quality of life of the West. But money doesn't eliminate loneliness. A poor Armenian woman may only be able to afford to cook potatoes every night for dinner, but still goes to bed every night in the loving embrace of a husband who adores her.

These issues of the soul can only be cared for by the one who created the soul. A broken heart is not healed by the salve of financial security, and emptiness cannot be filled with possessions.

C.S. Lewis, in his book *The Great Divorce*, wrote about a young artist who had no desire to make the journey to heaven. Lewis described a man who lost a once intimate love of God as he began to love his own creation. His love for his work was so strong that he no longer held a sense of wonder for the source of inspiration—the real world all around him and the one who created everything. When we get everything that we ask for, sometimes the gift takes the place in our heart that the giver once occupied. This satisfies us for a while, but eventually leaves us needing something more gracious and more beautiful than any thing this world has to offer.

My sister's birthday weekend is over now. Our grand shopping spree for fall sweaters was a success. As I try to stuff my new clothing in to my suitcase, I take time to think about the last days.

I have come to realize that you don't have to go far to help someone in need. American or Armenian, we all require love. We all need to believe that we are on earth for a purpose.

In a few hours, I board a plane at Chicago O'Hare airport. Surprisingly, even though I was only in the US for five days, I feel ready to return to Armenia.

I love the food here. I love the shopping on Michigan Avenue. I cherish my home culture. I *loved* surprising my sister and spending time with her. But my husband, my kids, my closest friends all now live on the other side of the world.

America, I love you. But, now it's time to go *home*.

Wherever your *home* is, there are people who need you to reach into their lives.

Notice them.

Find a way to brighten their day.

Remind them that they are not alone.

Life without Love: A True Story of an Armenian Woman

Sometimes it's a curse to be beautiful.

It was 1964, and when Anush walked the streets of Tbilisi, she caught the eye of many bachelors. Her exotic dark eyes, long eyelashes and high cheekbones accentuated a slender, yet curvy, frame.

The doorbell would ring several times a month, with yet another suitor, wearing his best clothing, his hair tamed with oil, pleading with her parents for their daughter's hand in marriage. That was the custom. But Anush was an affluent Armenian living in the ancient capital of Georgia, Armenia's neighbor to the north. Her father was a prominent doctor and her family managed a renowned Armenian theater.

Father would quickly extinguish any hope of marriage when a young Georgian suitor would plead for his daughter. Armenians only marry Armenians. Anush's mother recruited many young candidates, but Anush was young and didn't want to leave her loving father and their happy household.

It was a cold, fall afternoon. The seasons seemed to have changed instantly, and within a moment, Anush's life also abruptly changed with the sudden death of her father. As her father's body laid on a table in their living room, reality set in. Anush clutched his cold, folded hand and knew that with her father's absence, all life had been drawn out of her bright future as well. Guests filled their home, repeatedly bowing and wailing as the sorrowful music of the double-reeded duduk played. She would never forget the sound of sorrow.

After the burial, she returned home, and her footsteps echoed off the wooden floors. A new emptiness had filled her heart. Her mother was overcome with grief and the responsibility of providing for three children.

A few months passed and winter had arrived. The sunless days seemed to only aggravate Anush's mother. Mother's eyes were dark and heavy, as if the months of daily crying had caused pools of sorrow to gather in big circles under her lashes. Hours passed alone, in a bedroom once shared with her husband. Anush's mother called her into the vacant bedroom.

"I can't carry the burden of supporting you while you try to find your true love. I've decided. You have to marry. The next Armenian man who comes and asks for your hand in marriage will be your next husband. You have no choice."

Every night, she would pray to remain invisible to the Armenian bachelors who crossed her path. She hoped for love. But real beauty, such as Anush possessed, rarely goes unnoticed.

Anush was 18 years old when she caught the eye of an Armenian man, 14 years her senior. He was visiting from Yerevan, Armenia and had come to Georgia to meet the beautiful Armenian he had heard about. He was a successful mathematics and chemistry professor who wrote many of the standard university textbooks, but had failed to find a life-long companion worthy of his intellect and success.

One day Anush entered her front door and saw the conversation halt as she encountered her mother and this older Armenian professor in negotiations. She attempted to act uninterested and refused to show him the normal, expected rules of hospitality. She did not rush to boil a cup of coffee or reach for the family's best chocolates. She clenched her jaw, walked to her bedroom and began to pray for some sort of escape.

As suddenly as her father was taken from her, Anush was forced to pack up all of her fine clothing and begin the long train ride to her new home in Yerevan, Armenia.

Every young woman dreams of her wedding day, and Anush was no different. But now she found herself looking up and committing herself to completely unfamiliar eyes.

"I will be obedient. I will be obedient. I will be obedient," Anush chanted fulfilling an old Armenian wedding tradition. Her life of obedience has officially begun.

Through their years of marriage, Anush was submissive and made sure to fulfill the duties of an Armenian wife. She gave him three children and worked tirelessly to make sure the home was perfect. Her husband always returned home to a dinner table prepared and an emotionless kiss.

According to Armenian custom, she had not only married an unknown husband, but was required to live with his parents as well. She was responsible for cleaning every corner of the home, washing, ironing and folding every person's laundry and preparing all the family meals. Her life of affluence and freedom was now a mere memory, and she understood what it felt like to be in prison.

A decade passed, and Anush's only true joy was found in her three children—a boy and two girls. She loved watching them grow, and she had hoped that her mother's promise would come true, that she would eventually grow to love the man she was forced to marry and serve. She would kiss her husband and wait, even hope for, a spark of love. But every kiss, instead, remained a forced, emotionless duty.

Anush tried her best to find joy in her every day life. Her husband was a well-respected mathematician and professor in the highly esteemed Soviet education system. He was given a good salary and more than one home from the Communist party. But that all seemed to fall under the authority of his controlling, live-in mother. Although many families struggled under the Soviet regime, at least Anush could be confident that all of her needs would be met.

She was still beautiful and wore the latest fashions that her mother would send from her hometown in Georgia. Anush would be a radiant diversion walking down the gray, soot-filled streets of Yerevan. She kept her home spotless and loved hearing the rooms filled with her children's laughter.

Realizing she lost her free will when her promise of obedience echoed against the stone church walls on her wedding day, she longed to find freedom. One day, she decided that her living room needed a makeover. It took all of her strength to move the antique furniture and heavy wardrobe into their new places. She felt as if she had brought new life to the room and had exercised a little freedom in her own personal jail cell.

Her husband returned home, expecting dinner to be prepared and the table set for his arrival. Anush anxiously awaited for him to notice the renovation. He entered the living room and froze. His jaw tightened, and his fist clenched. Anush suddenly realized that she had taken her step of freedom too far. Suddenly, she was knocked to the ground as her husband's fist beat her repeatedly. Change was not allowed. That day, Anush learned that for her, freedom did not exist.

Years passed, and Anush remained a dutiful wife. Her husband began to lose his life-long battle with diabetes. He had always loved to look at numbers on a page as his mind would meticulously solve the most difficult of mathematical problems. But his sight had blurred, then disappeared. He realized that his greatest asset had been lost. Desiring to leave his mark in his chosen field, he enlisted Anush to write down his dictated thoughts into one final book.

She spent hours on a hard, wooden chair near his bedside and would force her hand to quickly capture, on paper, every word form her dying husband's mouth.

Anush was saddened to see her husband, a tall and robust man, wither away. The night before he died, Anush sat near his bedside and her lips were whispering silent prayers to God. He began to search for her hand and grabbed it firmly. She looked into blank eyes that were searching for something they would never see again.

"Tell me, Anush. Did you ever grow to love me?"

Out of compassion, she could have reassured him with a lie. But through years of marriage and obedient service, he had never cared to ask her this question before.

Her lips began to form a positive response, but then the bitterness from the years of lost freedom arose.

"No...No."

A few days later her home was filled with visitors, dressed in black, who had come to see the body of her husband. He was wearing his best suit and laid in a small wooden coffin on their dining room table. Huge floral arrangements filled with red and white carnations were left near the entrance to their apartment building, a sign to all that a deceased person lie within.

Anush felt numb as dozens of people entered her home and sat silently in a corner staring at her husband's body. Some would walk by shaking their heads and clicking their tongues as a physical sign that he was too young to die. Again the sad music of the duduk echoed in her ears.

After the death of her husband, 40 days of mourning followed. She wore black and visited the grave several times as required by tradition. Her mother-in-law was controlling during the life of her husband, but she became worse after the death of her favorite, doting son.

She had never liked Anush, the woman who took a portion of her son's heart away from her. As the widow, she had the right to inherit all of her husband's property. But, her mother-in-law insisted that Anush sign the property over to her teenage son. Obedient as always, she signed the papers, but years later, Anush would realize her mistake. Anush never imagined that her son had grown into a man that would make her feel like an unwanted guest in the home she and her husband had built. Her son, now married, took her room and Anush shared a small bedroom with her adult daughter. When long-time neighbors would knock on Anush's door for their daily tea and gossip, she never felt comfortable serving them on the dining table she had, for years, set for her husband.

After the collapse of the Soviet Union, Armenia's main nuclear power plant was closed down. It was a very harsh winter, and it was left for each family to find ways to heat their homes. Anush walked in to her husband's study with shelves lined with books he had written and carefully preserved. She filled box after box with his precious books, created a fire pit in their living room and burned them. Although he had not provided love for Anush, he had always provided for his family's every need. And now, even in his death, his work was helping them survive the bitter cold.

Those difficult years finally passed, and Anush was excited for the day when her son had finally saved enough money to bring home a refrigerator and a washing machine. After years of washing clothing by hand and storing food in an old safe on the cold balcony, Anush would finally be able to enjoy a respite from the years of chapped hands and lukewarm food.

The day the appliances were delivered was an exciting one. Anush spent all morning rearranging the kitchen furniture to make room for the wonderful new additions. The sparkling white, new appliances finally arrived and the family gathered around to be amazed by what technology could do. Each had a sense of pride that their home was now affluent enough to own such luxuries.

But Anush had forgotten that these familiar walls were now her son's home. Anush's daughter-in-law made it clear that these appliances were only to be used by her. The next morning Anush kneeled by her bathtub, washing clothing by hand, as she heard the whiz of the laundry machine spinning outside the door.

Anush's two daughters were now in their thirties and had inherited her undeniable beauty. Each girl had many suitors come and ask for their hand in marriage, but the girls had learned from their mother's story. They were not willing to marry for money, respect or to follow cultural norms. They were waiting for love.

In Armenia, waiting for love is not always an option. The greatest desire

Chapter 16: Life without Love

of nearly every woman is to marry young and have children. Many of their neighbors would gossip that Anush's daughters were old maids, unused and unwanted.

But Anush knew the beauty of freedom and true love. When her daughters would occasionally allow the gossip to penetrate their resolve to wait for love, she would look deep in their eyes, brush aside their hair with her delicate hand and reassure them. Nothing is more lonely than vacant kisses and a hollow heart. Nothing is more maddening then a life spent as a captive of someone else's plan. Nothing is more poisonous to the soul than the bitterness of a wasted life.

No, daughters.

Live the life you've always dreamed of.

Wait for the love that brightens your step.

Whisper your prayers to God that your life will not be like mine.

Part Four

Heroes

Chapter Seventeen

A Nation Full of Heroes

A rmenia is an ancient place. Noah's Mt. Ararat fills the southern sky, towering above an unforgiving countryside. The land is dotted with centuries-old monasteries, sleepy villages, and crumbling monuments. Stifling clouds of smoke spew from trucks and cars salvaged from Russia and Europe, kept alive by resourceful Armenian mechanics. Despite its rich history and landscape, Armenia remains a name that many of us once memorized for a high school world geography exam and soon forgot. But heroes often arise from the most forgotten places.

To us, every Armenian that plods on in the face of daily financial insecurity is a hero. Each Armenian that survived the dark years following the collapse of the Soviet Union is a hero. Armenia is a nation full of heroes.

They may never be heroes who are hailed by the Nobel Peace Prize, have a statue erected in a park or a portrait hanging in a museum. But the Armenians have stood in the face of extinction, century after century, clutching each other's hands, impassioned to preserve their faith and their families. I find their joy is impenetrable; their resolve is something I have never experienced.

As we spent countless evenings in the homes of the spiritual fathers of a rapidly expanding church movement, we realized that we were in the presence of God's battle-hardened heroes of the faith. This section is dedicated to the Christian pastors who survived the occupation of the Soviet Union and who gave everything to establish the kingdom of God among their people.

Chapter Eighteen

Pastor Artavazd

I can't imagine what the Armenian pastors thought when they first saw us. Our area director had been visiting Armenia for a few years and had built wonderful relationships. For over a year, these pastors anticipated the arrival of the first missionaries from one of the largest, and most respected missions organizations in the world.

It was a sunny day in June, and our new friend, Hovhannes, the owner of one of the largest sausage companies in Armenia, drove us to Lake Sevan. As we approached the lake, a group of 30 pastors stood, gathered near the coast, awaiting our arrival.

We stepped out, confident, but very young, Nick was twenty-six and I was a mere twenty-four years old.

Their hearts must have sunk a bit. What could such young people possibly offer us? They are the age of our children! We've survived the KGB, what experience do they have?

We could feel their disappointment, even through their welcoming hugs and kisses on the cheek. They had hoped for a true equal; a seasoned pastor. But instead, they got us.

In the midst of our young awkwardness and their quizzical glances, we saw something that reached in through our veil of insecurity like a shaft of sunlight—kind eyes. These eyes belonged to Artavazd. He immediately walked up to us with a big welcoming smile and an invitation. Until now, eight years later, I can still see the softness of his eyes and the kindness of his soul radiating through them.

"I want you to come and speak at my church. Does next week work? You can stay with my family for the weekend! We would love to have you."

This simple, generous act was a spark that would shape our journey in Armenia. We had spent years preparing for our life in missions, and we were finally going to minister in an Armenian church.

A week later, a twenty-year-old, green *Lada* (Russian-made car) approached our home. In the front sat Artavazd's wife, Gayaneh, and we squeezed into the backseat. It was a hot July day, one of those days where your legs feel glued to the vinyl seats.

We began our 45-minute journey to the city of Hrazdan. The windows were rolled down, my long hair blowing. The *Lada* seemed to struggle under the burden of the extreme heat. It would start, then stop. Gayaneh, who had a massive headache, would groan with each lurch of the vehicle.

Pastor Artavazd was always patient. He would get out of the car with a small smile on his face (his permanent demeanor), to open the hood and see what could be done to help his old mechanical friend endure the heat. The car would lug us up a hill, and then Pastor Artavazd would turn off the engine and let it glide down the other side.

Hrazdan is an industrial town nestled in hills at an elevation of about 6,000 feet. We rumbled through the city streets, weaving around enormous potholes that appeared to have been made by a meteor shower.

Nick often said that driving in Armenia is like driving in a video game: negotiating the bee hive of cars, outwitting the road police looking for a bribe, navigating through a maze of winding streets devoid of name markers. We passed the city center and suddenly the car veered toward the sidewalk. Pastor Artavazd eased the front wheels up to the curb, gave it some gas and climbed over, and down the other side on to an unseen dirt path.

We arrived at their home, and climbed eight floors to their Soviet-built apartment. It was our first experience in an Armenian home, and this was the perfect introduction.

Artavazd, Gayaneh and their seven children welcomed us warmly. We sat around the dinner table (filled with stuffed grape leaves, pilaf and homemade walnut candies) late into the evening as we learned to count in Armenian. They would laugh when we mispronounced sounds, but were patient and willing instructors. Two of Artavazd's daughters gave up their beds for us that night, and we slept in the warmth of the Armenian summer and this family's hospitality.

The next morning, Shushan, their 16-year-old daughter, was able to translate for us as I greeted the church and Nick preached his first sermon in Armenia. We found out later that we were the first native English speakers she'd ever met. Shushan eventually became one of the primary translators on our project to publish the first ever study Bible in the Armenian language.

This family completely amazes us. Pastor Artavazd and Gayaneh were church planters under the heavy-handed rule of the Soviet Empire. They would hold services, hidden in the forests or in their front living room. Their children grew up as ministers in the church. They sang, played piano and guitar, wrote worship songs, led discipleship groups, organized camps, and taught Bible classes.

Artavazd, as a young pastor, was not satisfied that there was a strong church in Hrazdan. On weekdays, he taught mathematics at the local school near his home, but in his spare time, he would travel to nearby towns and villages. Not always having the opportunity to travel by car or bus, Artavazd would walk miles along the dirt roads of the Armenian countryside. As his shoes gathered dust from the journey, he would pray and prepare for the next church service in the neighboring town.

By June 2011, when we left Armenia, the two churches that he continues to pastor in Hrazdan had a combined average attendance of over six hundred people. Many of the churches he planted in the surrounding towns are still thriving under the leadership that he raised up, some of them with attendance of over 1,000 people.

Here is a man that without seminary training or church start-up funds, and under the risk of imprisonment or worse, has become one of the founding fathers of the Armenian evangelical church.

What did he have? He had the love of Christ that radiated out through his every action, his every word. It was that kindness, love and generosity that I saw in his welcoming hazel eyes our first week in Armenia that changed life after life in his community.

His seven children experienced their father's sacrifice, and continue to follow and serve Christ despite any difficulty. His city and government officials know his name and can't find a negative word to say about him. Why should they? Artavazd has never said a negative word about another person.

We've met countless people who advertise to the world how great they are. Then there are the heroes of the faith that show the world who they are through their love without even trying. They walk into a room, and everyone senses something is different about them. It's the subtle, confident smile; the words that drip with wisdom and encouragement; the aura of peace in their demeanor; and that radiating kindness in their eyes.

They don't have riches or mesmerizing charisma, but they change their community, one by one, through one smile, one prayer, one deed, one life-giving word or one extremely kind glance.

Chapter Nineteen
Pastor Rubik

Rubik is a tireless, relentless, fearless man. With a young congregation of a few hundred souls, they scrapped and fought the religious persecution that punished anyone who rented a hall to them for their meetings. Determined to build their own building to freely worship in, they gathered enough money to purchase an acre of land on the outskirts of their suburb—colloquially called Bangladesh. Having secured the land and the rights to build, a miracle in itself, they launched into construction.

The men of the church gathered early each morning, and Rubik would lay out the day's plan. Leading the way, he grabbed 70-pound bags of cement and began mixing concrete by hand. Each member of the church had sacrificed to give so that building material could be purchased, but the money soon ran out. They had barely begun.

Early on the morning of their first day without funds, Rubik gave out instructions to each volunteer. Like every day before, Rubik sat in a crowded bus that took him to the open tents of the city's outdoor construction market. With no money in the bank and nothing in his pockets, he placed the order for building material and trusted that God would be faithful.

On his way back to the site, while waiting for the material to arrive, the money came. Every day after, for 30 straight days, the same ritual would unfold. The work would begin, the order placed in faith, and exactly enough money would arrive. One day the necessary funds were given by another church, the next from a businessman. Often the day's work was funded by many people dropping off their offerings early in the morning; returning home knowing they had played a part in building their church.

On the 30th day, a Sunday, the men who worked throughout the night to build wooden benches walked out of the building at 11 a.m. as the congregation filed in. Pastor Rubik stood in front of his congregation, on their new platform, built by their hands, and worshipped with tears flowing freely down his face.

This is the first church that we worshiped in on our very first Sunday in Armenia. This is where we met our wonderful friend, Marina. Today, Emmanuel church worships in a much larger building built right next to that little chapel. Over a thousand people crowd in every Sunday and hope for a seat. Another three-story education wing was subsequently built. The miracles continue. We will never forget the miraculous faith of this hero, our friend, Pastor Rubik.

Chapter Twenty
Pastor Baris

It was a particularly cold day in the mountains of Aragatsotn. A small crowd stood around a grave where a Kurdish man was about to be buried underneath its metal roof. Each family member poured a handful of soil and symbolically covered the casket with the finality of burial, a life underground.

Baris stood there among the guests, disturbed by the meaninglessness of life as yet another fellow villager lay lifeless. This ominous question had bothered him for a long time. Life in the Kurdish village felt like every day tumbled into the next—nothing to fill your time; nothing to hope for.

The Kurds are a nationless people group living as a minority—primarily in Iraq and Turkey. In Armenia, they live in the remote regions where healthcare is poor and infrastructure ends kilometers from their mountain villages. They live off the land, and with few trees growing on the plateau, they heat their homes with cow dung during the long winters. Many of the men were forced to find work in Russia, and those who remained accepted the few undesirable jobs left in the nation.

Was this life? Baris spent years trying to find something to believe in; to give meaning to his life. Finally, he discovered that everything felt better when he had a bottle of vodka nearby. He would start drinking early in the morning and would be drunk by afternoon. This was his daily routine.

By the end of the day, the vodka could no longer keep his hopelessness at bay, and he would begin to beat his wife. He had hoped that each fist full of anger would expend even a fraction of his inner anguish. But each night as he laid his head on his pillow next to his crying and bruised wife, he only felt more alone and wallowed in complete regret.

As was custom among the Kurds, he returned to the gravesite and helped one of his closest friends, Pashik, construct the metal roof and elaborate fence that would surround his father's grave. As they worked all day under the pounding rays of the sun, Baris listened as Pashik argued with another Kurish man.

"Pashik. What's the point of life when we all will eventually go to hell anyway? There is no salvation for the Kurds."

Pashik looked over at Baris, and as he spoke, Baris realized his childhood friend's life had been changed.

"But there is hope through Jesus Christ. True—we're all sinners, but His death has brought us forgiveness. Jesus is not only the Savior of the Armenian Christians. He is the Savior of you and me—if we ask!"

Baris' stiff shoulders sunk down as if the burden he had been carrying finally became too great. He was aware, more than ever, that he was in great need of some sort of a savior. Baris followed Pashik home that night to learn more, and he walked home with a Bible.

Baris was skeptical. The Yezdi Kurds believed in a God and knew many of the ancient stories from the Old Testament of the Bible. They even knew who Satan was and would offer sacrifices to Satan in order to appease him and keep his evil away from their fragile existence. But he had never heard of Jesus before.

The story of Jesus' life and death haunted Baris as he returned home that day. He wanted to cast his friend's words aside as nothing more than a fairy tale, but his mind and soul longed for any form of hope. So Baris read the words of the New Testament every day through the foggy lens of the vodka—his constant companion.

One evening, Baris sat outside his home with his tattered Bible. He had turned to the book of John and finally understood the meaning of a verse: "For God so loved the world, that He gave His only son so that whoever believes in Him, will not die, but will have eternal life." (John 3:16)

As he threw rock after rock at a target on his fence, he lifted up a prayer to Jesus. He was willing to try anything.

Jesus. Forgive me. Save me. If you are real, deliver me from alcohol. Take away my desire to drink. If you do this miracle, I will know you are real.

Baris went straight to bed that night. If Jesus had done anything, at least his thoughts had kept him from beating his wife.

He awoke the next day and felt different. He looked over at the bottle, and his hand reached for his daily habit. Then he remembered his prayer, and he paused to see if something inside him had changed. Minutes passed by, and the urge to guzzle what alcohol he had left wasn't there. It was clear. He did not want a drink. He sat the bottle back down, still believing that he wouldn't make it to lunchtime without a sip.

Lunch came. He didn't want vodka. Dinner passed. It came time for bed, and his wife was given a second day without a beating. As Baris fell asleep that night, he knew that tomorrow would most likely be different. He would need a drink. Still once again he offered his challenge to Jesus for another day.

As day after day passed, Baris regained a part of himself and his life had more clarity as he threw out the bottles of vodka in the pantry. His desire was completely gone, and his life began to change. Everyone in the village noticed that he was a new man. Other hopeless Kurds came to him, hoping to learn the secret to his newfound joy and freedom. Baris' answer was always the same—he had found a Savior, Jesus.

As Baris looked out over the homes in his village, he realized the great responsibility he had to share the story of Jesus with his fellow Kurdish neighbors. He began to visit each home and shared the stories from the Old Testament that they all knew and revealed how those old stories foretold of a coming Savior, Jesus Christ. Many, like Baris, decided to follow Jesus Christ.

Baris' wife, Naziko, did not. She was a part of the family of a Yezdi shaman. If she accepted Christ it would bring shame on her family, but she saw the inexplicable change in Baris' life. One evening while begrudgingly bowing her head to pray with Baris, she looked up and saw Jesus, in excruciating pain, dying on a cross. Through the agony, Jesus looked at her and said, "I did this for you."

That night, Naziko joined Baris in the journey as a follower of Christ.

Baris, with his limited knowledge of the Bible, started a church in that Kurdish community. He didn't realize it was a church, nor did he set out to start a church. But his focus was to share the life-changing hope he had experienced. A group of Christians began to gather in his home, and they explored the Bible and grew together.

Years later, a large home in the village was purchased and renovated as a place to meet. The bottom floor was painted in bright colors and used as a preschool where children could come, learn and be given a warm meal. It was the only preschool for Kurdish children in their community.

The second floor eventually became a meeting hall, complete with long wooden benches and a keyboard. And each Sunday morning, to this day, amidst the cold mountains of the Aragatsotn plateau, the walls echo with the voices of over 150 Kurds who gather to sing and worship God.

Baris has received death threats, and there have been many attempts to take his life because of his dedication to Christ. But his resolve remains strong, and for years, his church in the mountains of Armenia was the largest Kurdish church in the world. He continues to tirelessly visit the homes in his community and has gained respect as a blessing to his people.

Baris can always be seen driving his white, Russian-made jeep throughout the Kurdish villages of Armenia or sitting on an airplane traveling to nearby countries teaching new Kurdish Christians how to reach their nation with the hope of Christ.

Chapter Twenty One

Pastor Hovik and Lusine

The first time we entered their home and took a seat at their dining room table, we knew that we had met life-long friends. After a long Sunday service, we all had a similar look and feeling of exhaustion.

Lusine, nine months pregnant, had led worship. Hovik smiled and greeted all of his church members and then finished all of his behind-the-scene pastoral tasks and demands. I sang that morning at the church, then worked to entertain Oliver, still a toddler, during the two-hour service. Nick preached and prayed for many. Now it was time for a much-deserved meal, finished with cups of welcomed tea and coffee.

Entering their home, Lusine quickly took off her heels and let her aching feet rest in a comfortable pair of house slippers. She placed a crystal bowl, filled with chocolate, on the table and hurried to the kitchen to prepare a Sunday meal.

Lusine looked tired as she cooked, but I could also feel her excitement as we discussed the fulfillment of one of her dreams—to hold another baby in her arms. Only a few days of a long pregnancy remained.

Nick and Hovik quickly bonded, and their laughter could be heard resounding throughout the apartment. We were all of a similar age on a similar journey. We all wanted to establish God's church in Armenia. But none of us could imagine the difficulty that awaited Hovik and Lusine.

With our bellies full of Armenian flatbread, lavash, and barbequed pork (an Armenian specialty), we got in our car and began the 90-minute drive back to Yerevan. Lusine smiled and waved as we drove away, but as soon we were out of sight, she reached for her husband. She did not feel well and had not felt the baby move all day.

Throughout the Sunday morning service and meal, she would console her worry.

Everything will be fine. The baby is just sleeping. I am moving a lot and just not taking the time to notice the baby's movement.

But a mother's heart can always sense the struggle of her child. She felt, deep down, that something wasn't right. So they drove to the nearest hospital and were immediately seen by a doctor. After an ultrasound, the doctor told Lusine that everything was fine. He quickly sent her home, told her to return in three days for her scheduled C-section and wished her a happy delivery.

Lusine trusted the doctor against her own instincts and convinced herself that her worry was just a sign of her exhaustion and anticipation. A few days later, Lusine waddled up the steps to the hospital. In a few short hours she would hold her little Daniella. She laid down on the table as the doctor worked to find a heartbeat. She held her breath when she saw the doctor's strained expression. He was pushing the baby, pulling on her skin, applying more gel to her round belly. He attempted to look calm.

"Sometimes these instruments are inaccurate. We'll go to the ultrasound room. They should be able to find the heartbeat. Everything will be just fine."

He patted her shoulder and quickly left the room.

As Lusine laid down on the table in the dark room, she closed her eyes and whispered a quick prayer. But the picture on the computer screen couldn't lie. There was no heartbeat. There laid her beautiful baby, curled up in her mother's womb, but life had slipped away.

Lusine cried out with the realization that this baby, which she had carried and loved for 40 weeks, would never get to feel the warmth of a kiss on her cheek or experience the joy she would have brought to their family.

A Caesarian section went as scheduled, and Lusine's beautiful baby was taken. The surgery was traumatic, and Lusine's spirit was crushed. She was wheeled into a room filled with other patients for a three-day recovery. The grief and emptiness she experienced was so severe that she fell into a pit of despair.

Lusine woke up in the early hours of the morning alone in her bed. Tears flowed as she remembered the way things should've been. She should be waking up early to feed her newborn, and not alone in this cold room full of strangers.

Lusine read her Bible in search of peace. She sang songs of worship in her heart to a God that she knew was faithful despite her circumstances.

She even began to console the woman next to her, who felt completely hopeless, too. As she ministered, the woman could tangibly feel and sense the peace that Lusine had in God and desired to experience that same peace. With an amazing strength and generosity, in the face of great loss, Lusine prayed for the woman.

"Imagine how great our God is that even during this time of personal distress, I still share about His love."

Lusine repeated this challenge many times as patients throughout the clinic would find a way to Lusine's bedside. They, too, were looking for hope.

Lusine's recovery was far from easy. Her body mended quickly, but her spirit required months of healing. She often blamed herself for trusting a doctor and returning home when she *knew* in her heart that there was a problem. Lusine regretted her personal desire to study, work and provide for her family's every need during her pregnancy rather than allowing herself to relax and enjoy the miracle. But at every cringe and regret of her heart, she was always met with an unbelievable sense of peace and hope.

Hovik and Lusine had already lived a life of hoping against all hope. In their mid-twenties, they were sent out from their home church to restart a church in a difficult, unreached area in the city of Vanadzor. The poverty in that area was great. They worked tirelessly to become a part of their new community. Their home was always filled with guests for tea, and their phone was always ringing with a request to help someone in need.

Little by little, they began to build a thriving group of Christian believers in that area. Hovik's friendly smile and Lusine's fiery personality helped them quickly integrate as an indispensable part of their neighborhood. After meeting in their small apartment building and filling it with dozens of chairs for their weekly home services, they rented an old store. Nearly every day they would walk to church on a main road that climbed through their community and ended halfway up the side of a small mountain. They crammed nearly a hundred people into the small meeting hall and soon needed more room.

Hovik shared his vision to purchase a building that had been under construction but abandoned half finished. Offerings were taken, and he was speechless as he watched widowed grandmas throw their gold rings and jewelry into the offering bag. He knew the people in his church had given everything possible. Desperate for funds, Hovik hiked into the forested mountains surrounding Vanadzor, collected firewood, and sold it house to house. Exhausted, he now had 100 dollars in his pocket. Realizing he could never do this himself, he asked God to perform a miracle.

Stepping out in faith, Hovik made a call the next week and scheduled an appointment with the mayor of the city. He entered city hall with a prayer on his lips and one hundred dollars in his pocket. He brushed off his dusty shoes, straightened his suit coat and entered the mayor's office. Hovik gritted his teeth as he waited to hear the mayor's response.

"Well, I have some property that is city-owned, and we have not been able to sell it. I'd just be happy if it would be used. If I give you that property at city auction price, do you think you could raise the funds to construct your church building?"

Hovik nearly jumped out of his chair. He eagerly began to shake the mayor's hand and promised that he would build a church building worthy of the city's generosity. He walked out of the door, and the clerk handed him a contract that stated the price of the land on the front page: $3,500.

He prayed the whole way home, not sure if he had just walked himself off of a cliff or just witnessed the greatest miracle of his life. The property would have cost ten times that amount on the open market, considering that a foundation had already been dug and built in the perfect size for his church.

He began calling all of the elders in the church, rejoicing at what had just happened. By the end of the day, a church member, who had just returned form Russia, dropped off the $3,500. They finalized the purchase and began dreaming of what they could build.

Years have passed since Hovik signed the papers on that piece of land. His church building has been built, brick by brick, by the extreme generosity of his church and Christians from all around the world.

Even in the midst of building, Hovik and Lusine's church has continued to grow and thrive. I will never forget Hovik's large grin and the wisdom in his words. I will never fail to remember Lusine's strong spirit and desire for a child.

Hovik and Lusine have not only made an impact on their community but faithfully make the long treks through unpaved roads to villages that have no church. They gather in a small home and share the tangible love of Christ with those hungry for hope.

Hovik and Lusine have needed grace, and they have seen it poured out. They have needed hope and longed for joy. At every turn, their God has been there to sustain them.

They have worked to build a church—not just constructed of walls, but filled with people—and God is building it through them.

"And now I'm going to tell you who you are, really are. You are Peter, a rock. This is the rock on which I will put together my church, a church so expansive with energy that not even the gates of hell will be able to keep it out."
—Matthew 16:18, The Message

Chapter Twenty Two
Pastor Mikaiel

When Mikaiel was a young man, he loved to go to school and especially cherished his science books. His teachers noticed his hunger to learn biology, chemistry and physics.

Since the Soviet government was told to keep their eye out for students with great potential, Mikaiel was eventually identified as a great mind who deserved the best education available. As he made his way through school, he proved his immense intellect and it was decided that he would become a Soviet scientist.

What they didn't expect was that his best friend and fellow science protégé, Samvel, challenged him with the story of Christ. Knowing that science didn't hold all the secrets of the universe, Mikaiel knew, without a doubt, that he would choose to follow God.

Now one of the best students in the university's science program, everyone was impressed by his mastery of all subjects and he became an influential leader among his classmates. He compelled many of his friends to follow Christ and led a weekly Bible study under the watchful eye of the secret police.

Months passed, and Mikaiel noticed that something had changed. His once-attentive professors looked at him suspiciously and held their distance. He was soon called away from his science lab and taken to small room. He waited with a sense of dread.

Sitting before him was a KGB agent who had been sent from Moscow to deal with this growing "Christian problem" in the Science University in Armenia. The agent's words were few, but powerful nonetheless. The man began quoting scripture from memory, mocking what he himself had once believed as a young man. Mikaiel felt an intense presence of evil in the room, like he was face to face with the devil himself.

"This is what you will do. You will sign this paper that says you are rejecting Christianity and admit to your errors. This will be distributed throughout the university and among your fellow students. And, this problem—*your* problem—will go away and you will be allowed to continue your training. If you refuse to sign this document, you will be immediately exiled to Siberia. Either way, this problem will go away. I will be back tomorrow and we will meet here again."

That night Mikaiel didn't sleep as he paced back and forth in his small, cold dormitory bedroom. The decision was impossible to make. His quick mind raced as it played out different scenarios, trying to discover new solutions. Despite all the calculations, desperate prayers and immobilizing fear, Mikaiel knew what he would do. Morning dawned and Mikaiel approached his day with a sense of dread. He knew what awaited him in that small dark room at the university. The queasiness in his stomach wouldn't allow him to eat.

When he arrived at the university, he felt as if each heavy step was a step closer to a destiny he wished he could avoid. Throughout the morning, he pretended to listen to the lectures, but he was waiting. Just waiting.

Hours passed and no one called for him. The appointed time for his meeting had come and gone. Finally, one of his head professors approached and asked Mikaiel to follow him.

Mikaiel's footsteps echoed loudly in his ears as he walked through the familiar hallways. The professor led him to his personal office and asked Mikaiel to sit in the wooden chair opposite him.

"Mikaiel, we all know who came to visit you yesterday. Today when the driver went to pick him up from his hotel, they found him dead. No one knows what happened. You are free to go. Be careful."

Mikaiel left that small office in shock. Tears began to uncontrollably flow down his cheeks. He had stared in the face of the Soviet Union, and he survived.

Mikaiel continued to study and continued to share his hope in God. When it came time for him to receive his Doctorate, Moscow finally found a way to punish him. Because of his unwavering faith in God, he was denied his Doctoral certification.

Mikaiel can now be found in the north of Armenia, leading more than a 1,000 Christians every Sunday. Despite offers to run for Parliament, Mikaiel has chosen to pastor in the north of Armenia and lead a union of churches, continuing to help Armenians find hope in a true Savior, his Savior.

Part Five

A Turn
in the Road

Chapter Twenty Three
Ashland Avenue

As a teenager, I hated running. Every year I would dread the day when my school's gym teacher would time us as we ran the mile. I was anxious standing at the starting line, just waiting for the coach to blow her whistle as she stared down at her stopwatch.

I was in junior high, and we were forced to sport unflattering gym uniforms. Slender girls would prance by in their bright red shorts and blue t-shirts like they were born to run. I would try to drag myself and the excess 25 pounds I carried in my belly and thighs around the track. Run, then walk. Run again and witness the tiny, popular girl speed by, then continue walking with a feeling of defeat. I dreaded being one of the last people to cross the finish line. There was no warm reception or cheers, just a group of young girls chatting with each other and stopping long enough to toss a questioning glance my way, "*What took you so long?*"

My freshman year of high school only escalated the pressure. The halls seemed filled with handsome football players and cheerleaders in mini-skirts. In my fourteen-year-old mind, it didn't seem fair. I was motivated to change. At first, I could only run two or three blocks. Then I'd stop, walk and start over. Every day, I would run a bit further. My unquenchable desire to achieve eventually took over and within a few months, I was running four miles every day.

I grew up in Saint Joseph, Missouri—a mid-sized, mid-western city. This was the hometown of the outlaw Jesse James and the Pony Express, America's first mail system. My home was a three-story Victorian house sitting where Felix Street crested on its way downtown. My family had moved to this quiet, old neighborhood when I was only four years old to escape the crime-riddled section of Kansas City where I was born.

My four-mile run was the same every day. I would run down Felix Street to Noyes Avenue. Noyes was a mile-long hill that emptied onto beautiful Ashland Avenue.

Ashland was lined with old, gingerbread-like homes. Its mature trees would cast shadows over bicycles, cars, and passersby. Unrelenting roots of maple and oak unseated concrete slabs of sidewalk and curb, creating a mystical, inimitable charm.

I would run past Ashland's graveyard. Its border was traced by a black, wrought iron fence, and a tall brick archway stood at the entryway. In this graveyard were the founders of the city and prominent families that once resided on Ashland Avenue.

My feet graced Ashland's paths in the hot, humid Missouri summers. I pounded the pavement and kicked away leaves in the crisp fall. My lungs burned as I inhaled the cold winter air and carefully avoided patches of ice. I would jump over the puddles pooling on the uneven sidewalk during the Spring. I experienced Ashland Avenue during every stage of the year. Ashland Avenue experienced its residents in every stage of life.

I have a connection to this road. Ashland was there for me during those painful years of growing. She supported my steps of healing as I overcame physical difficulties that resulted from the anorexia that defined my first years of high school. She was there for me as I learned to lean on my family, friends, and my faith. I enjoyed her unchanging soul that never wavered in her faithfulness. As I continue to run down the path of my life, I can look back and imagine the footprints I left there, and know that she is proud to have been part of the canvas on which my story has been painted.

My family's career in missions was a turn in the path that I never expected. But as I have continued to place one foot in front of the other, I have seen this has truly been the path that God designed. There have been so many times when I have fought to jump off the path—to follow after the easier route, to run into one of those beautiful homes on Ashland Avenue where I can nestle up in the safety of the known and pursue selfish dreams.

There are days when I feel like the race has gotten too intense and I am gasping for air. Gasping for freedom. Gasping to be in some other stage of life that doesn't involve so much maintenance and responsibility. I am writing this book in between gasps and hoping that something beautiful and life changing arises.

I first dreamed of writing about Ashland Avenue during a typical day's run when I was 17 years old and preparing to graduate from high school and embark on a new life, away from home and the comfortable streets of St. Joseph. Now, 16 years later, I am finally able to write this story and the stories of our life in Armenia.

Eight years after we first landed in Armenia, we once again entered the airport to leave our home in Yerevan and embark on a new road that God has expertly designed. We look back on the struggles, the accomplishments and the friendships we experienced in Armenia, and we see a few extra gray hairs on our heads and marvel at the beauty of the journey.

As I write the conclusion of this book, I sit in my new apartment in Tallinn, Estonia. Four weeks ago, today, we arrived in a new country—our new home. Yesterday was our first Estonian language lesson, and I left the crowded, stuffy university room feeling overwhelmed, head pounding and stomach in knots. As Nick and I dream of our mission here, to plant a church and start a church planting network, we feel like those young, inexperienced missionaries who landed in Yerevan years ago.

When I landed in that crumbling Soviet airport, He was there. When I sat on my balcony, just longing to return home to America, He was there. When I stood on a stage in front of hundreds of women or in the house of a forgotten Kurdish woman, He was there.

My journey took me along Ashland Avenue, turned down the streets of Yerevan, and continues down the cobblestone paths of Tallinn. In every language lesson, in every ministry event, in every challenging decision, in every conversation, He makes this promise—

"I am *there*."

Acknowledgements

Thank you to my wonderful husband, Nick. This book is a reality because you believed in it and tirelessly encouraged me to pursue a dream. Thanks for dragging me to Armenia and challenging me to love deeper and experience the true adventure of a life given away.

Thank you to my children, Oliver and Ava. You are the true treasures of my life. This book is also written for you. May you never forget the nation that loved you so dearly during the first years of your lives!

Thank you to our leadership: Omar and Pat; Norm and Heather. You have helped make our ministry dreams come true. You lead with excellence and wisdom. Your words and actions have impacted and inspired us.

Thank you to my parents, Kent and Leslie. You have been my life-long guides and encouragers. Thanks for raising this serious and stubborn soul, and for being an example of how to be true to myself, my faith and giftings. Much I learned about writing, I learned from you. Mom, thanks for the hours and days you spent editing my thoughts. You truly are gifted and a part of this story belongs to you!

Thank you to my sister, Hilary. You are my one constant, life-long, witty friend—and for that I am extremely grateful.

Thank you to Jasmina, our Armenian language teacher. Your love and open heart sustained us through the difficult first year. Your and Andranik's friendship is one of our greatest riches from Armenia.

Thank you to Anahit, our Armenian language teacher. You opened your home, heart and knowledge of the Armenian language to us. We are so grateful.

Thank you to Marina, our most trusted companion and my best friend in Armenia. We would never have made it through those eight years without you. Thank you for watching my kids during the many final hours I dedicated to this book.

Thank you to the Ghazaryan family. Your love and acceptance was a lifeline in Armenia.

Thank you to Pastor Karen and Tsogher. Your sermons inspired us and your encouraging, wise words helped us run the race in Armenia.

Thank you to Vahram and Arpine. You helped us bring humanitarian aid to the most needy in Armenia and showed us what true Armenian hospitality is like.

Thank you to our wonderful Armenian ministry partners and friends. You are the true heroes. You know who you are and we love you! A special thanks to Pastor Rubik Tumanyan, Pastor Rafael Grigoryan and Pastor Artur Simonyan for opening up the doors of ministry for us in Armenia.

Thank you to Jim and Eloise Neely. Your companionship, understanding heart and wisdom sustained us through our first term. Thanks for letting us live in your Yerevan home too!

Thank you to Hovhannes, the good Samaritan. You opened every door and gave yourself completely to us so that we could live and work in Armenia.

Thank you to my sisterhood of expat and American friends. You helped me and my kids survive and flourish overseas.

Thank you to all of our supporters and friends in ministry. We could not do anything without your giving, your prayers and your expertise. This is your adventure too!

14631631R00069

Made in the USA
Charleston, SC
22 September 2012